RESPONSIVE DESIGN WORKFLOW

STEPHEN HAY

New Riders

VOICES THAT MATTER™

RESPONSIVE DESIGN WORKFLOW
Stephen Hay

New Riders
www.newriders.com
To report errors, please send a note to errata@peachpit.com
New Riders is an imprint of Peachpit, a division of Pearson Education.

Project Editor: Michael J. Nolan
Production Editor: Rebecca Winter
Development Editor: Margaret S. Anderson/Stellarvisions
Copyeditor: Gretchen Dykstra
Proofreader: Patricia Pane
Indexer: Jack Lewis
Cover & Interior Designer: Charlene Charles-Will
Compositor: Danielle Foster

ISBN 13: 978-0-321-88786-3
ISBN 10:   0-321-88786-7

9 8 7 6 5 4 3 2 1

Printed and bound in the United States of America

FOR MARJOLEIN, COLIN, CHRISTOPHER, SARAH, AND LEX.

Acknowledgements

Writing a book is hard (let's go shopping). And while this isn't a big book, I'm amazed at how much work—by so many people—has gone into it.

I'd like to thank Michael Nolan, who saw writing potential in me nine years ago, and again last year when I finally had the mental space to jump into the deep end and try. A friendly man with impeccable taste in authors.

A huge thanks to Margaret Anderson, Secret Weapon of Authors™, who was this book's emergency power supply. Margaret is half psychologist, half development editor, half mental coach, and half project manager. But wait, you say. That's four ha—yup. Indeed. Margaret made my first trek into book-writing territory as painless as it could be. It only hurts when I laugh.

Thanks also to copy editor Gretchen Dykstra, who spiced up all my boring black text by adding red. Lots and lots of red. Gretchen taught me lots about the English language, especially the fact that I don't know how to write it. I think it should become public knowledge that authors are only as good as their copy editors.

A huge thank you to Charlene Will for this book's design. Also Rebecca Winter, Patricia Pane, Danielle Foster, Jack Lewis, and the rest of the Peachpit/New Riders team. An incredible amount of work done by a bunch of friendly and talented people.

But that's not all. Oh, no, that's not all. Many thanks to . . .

Jake Archibald, eerily talented developer, for agreeing to tech edit this book for me. I chose him because of his superior knowledge, friendly demeanor, and politically incorrect humor. He repaid me by telling me that my JavaScript should be more *JavaScripty*. What does that even mean? He's an oracle.

Ana Nelson, author of Dexy, which now plays an important role in my work. Thanks to Ana for spending suspicious amounts of time with me on Skype answering all of my questions, and even adding stuff to Dexy so it could accommodate my bizarre use cases. She even taught me a little Python along the way. I'm the first official Ana Nelson fanboy; group therapy awaits.

Ethan Marcotte, distinguished gentleman of web design, for his wonderful foreword. He has inspired me for years.

Tim Kadlec, who had just finished his book and was my big example and took all my questions gracefully. Bruce Lawson, for recommending the Secret Weapon™. Aarron Walter, Mike Rohde, and Travis Holmes for their image contributions.

And all those who have inspired my work—whether they know it or not—in person, online, during conversations, or through their great work. These include Stephanie and Bryan Rieger, Jeremy Keith, Scott Jehl, Christian Heilmann, Remy Sharp, Brad Frost, Lyza Danger Gardner, Karen McGrane, Jason Grigsby, Kristina Halvorson, Peter-Paul Koch, Krijn Hoetmer, Jennifer Robbins, Robert Jan Verkade, Marrije Schaake, Bert Bos, Luke Wroblewski, Vasilis van Gemert, and many, many others. I'm privileged to call some of these people my friends.

My mother and my sister, of course, who are always encouraging, and to my father, who would have loved to see this book come to be.

My beautiful, wonderful kids, for having lost some free time with me and for having put up with some serious moodiness on my part.

And finally, Marjolein, my partner in crime. Her support, advice, love, and encouragement are ultimately the reason these words are in print.

Contents

3 Content Reference Wireframes 25

4 Designing in Text   51

5 Linear Design   69

8   Creating a Web-Based Design Mockup   125

II Creating Design Guidelines **187**

Foreword
by Ethan Marcotte

I have to be blunt: this is a wonderful book you're about to read.

There's a quote by Ludwig Wittgenstein that I've always loved: "The limits of my language are the limits of my world." Something's always seemed magical about that image: the broader your vocabulary, the broader your horizons.

I think of it often, especially as I remember my first studio job. Because looking back, I realize my introduction to web design was, well, pretty narrow, framed as it was by four little words: discover, design, develop, and deploy. Those were, I was taught, the discrete, task-based phases into which each design project was segmented. Research preceded design, and then coding followed, leading to site launch. Simple. Straightforward. Linear.

That model of working felt a bit like a relay race: teams would have to finish their work before the next could begin, handing work down the line before a site could launch. Of course, the truth was often quite a bit messier. And as we began designing beyond the desktop, bringing our work to more and more screens, that old, linear workflow began to show its limitations. Teams need to collaborate more; research, design, and development are more closely related than we once thought, and that old waterfall method kept them siloed.

Thankfully, in these pages, Stephen shares his years of thinking about a more web-native, responsive design process. And as he leads us from design exercises, to a new mode of wireframing, to introducing clients to responsive design, one thing becomes clear: this is a better way to work.

If the limits of our world *are* set by our language, then Stephen's book is a veritable dictionary: one full of concepts and techniques to reinvent the way you think about not only design, but the web in general.

This book is going to make your world so much wider. Enjoy.

IN SPLENDID VARIETY THESE CHANGES COME

"*Not everything is design.*
But design is about everything.
So do yourself a favor: be ready for anything."
—MICHAEL BIERUT

The web is a place of constant change, innovation, and well, wonder. The things we can do on, with, and because of the web are absolutely amazing, particularly when you remember what the early days of the commercial web were like. Thinking about the early days, the way we built websites in 1995 and what design possibilities were available to us then—it all seems laughable now.

In some ways, the web design process is completely different today, but in others, it's exactly the same.

Designers have scrambled since the beginning of the commercial web to translate the ideas in their heads to the browser. The first popular web designers were those clever enough to devise hacks that helped to achieve this goal. From spacer GIFs and layout tables to sliding doors, faux columns, and image replacement, to frameworks, CSS preprocessors, and JavaScript polyfills, we've traveled through a whole spectrum of creative ways to get our designs onto the web, even if that meant breaking the semantic web in the process, by combining our content with meaningless presentational elements.

And yet, while people, devices, browsers, and the entire web have changed, design processes have remained largely the way they've been since the very beginning of the web—even *before* the web, actually.

The birth of static hi-fi mockups

I used to work in print design. I graduated a few months before moving from the United States to the Netherlands. It took me weeks of calling every creative agency in the phone book in my area before one called me back and—after an interview—offered me the chance to be an intern. This was 1992, three years before most of the general public in the Netherlands was offered commercial internet access. The small agency had one desktop computer; I believe it was an Apple Macintosh LC. It was not for design. It was for things like writing letters and creating invoices. Design proposals were drawings, done by hand with very expensive colored markers.

That's how we designed things. We drew them, just as I'd been taught in college: create thumbnail sketches (the more the better), then make a selection. From that selection, make some rough sketches. From the best of those, choose between one and three—usually it was three because ad agencies loved to do tons of work in hopes of reeling in the account—and work that out in the best visualization possible. At the time, marker renderings were still top dog. Prepress work was outsourced in whole or in part to specialized agencies. Having worked with computers quite a bit as a student, I was surprised that they weren't utilized as much in the industry. But that changed quickly.

I was hired six months later. My pet love for typography led me to find ways to use QuarkXPress on the company's Macintosh Quadra 700 (bought quite soon after my internship started) to set type, print it out, and draw on top of it, incorporating real type into marker renderings. This made things much more realistic for our clients and gave them a more accurate impression of what they were getting. Other designers I knew did the same thing. We started incorporating color-printed images into our design impressions instead of drawing them. It wasn't long before I started using a combination of Photoshop and QuarkXPress to create complete mockups on the screen. I did a lot of packaging design, and I felt pretty smart doing everything on the computer, printing it out and then drawing shadows and such on top of the print with markers, until I started doing all of it in Photoshop because it all looked so *real*. Clients loved that type of rendering, and the more experienced marker renderers we used to outsource to stopped getting work from us altogether.

I felt fantastic about what I was doing, but failed to notice that it was taking me longer and longer to do what I used to do with markers in a fraction of the time. I was creating a product instead of visualizing an idea. However, after all the work involved, if we did get an account, some of what I'd done actually saved me production time. Lots of copy was typeset, and layout was essentially finished. Besides, this way of working was becoming the norm. When I first started doing Photoshop comps, it was pretty normal to pitch against agencies that still did everything by hand. And we won almost every time, because clients had the feeling they knew what they were getting. Eventually, everyone did it this way.

Interesting discussions ensued. Were we as designers *less creative* because we used new tools? The impression was that markers on paper were somehow an extension of our creativity, while computers stifled or stole that creativity to some extent. Did the computer as a visualization tool in fact make us less creative? Or did we simply have a more effective way of visualizing our already creative ideas? What about the time investment, especially in an industry that took—and still takes—spec work for granted? Was it really necessary to visualize in so much detail in the presale phase?

Like it or not, that's the way things went. Clients had come to expect high-quality, high-fidelity prints of design ideas. We still pasted these on presentation board, which was really the only way to say, "Hey, this is just a proposal, an impression." But we couldn't knock it, because for print, visuals from a computer *are* closer to reality than marker drawings.

The static mockup comfort zone

After we'd been making hi-fi static mockups for print work for a couple of years, a funny thing happened. The web was born. One might expect this collection of world-changing technologies to catalyze changes in process similar to the way design had moved from manual rendering to computer-aided rendering. *But everything stayed the same.* We stuck with Photoshop comps. We made pretty pictures of what we were going to make later. And clients accepted it. And we've worked that way for years.

Think about this for a minute: the changes in design that came about with the rise of desktop publishing were geared toward making designs more realistic. They were showing—more accurately than ever before—what the end product would look like. Why didn't that same shift happen when the web came along?

I have my pet theories, one of which is that some things just weren't as nice on the web. In the early days, type was not anti-aliased. Photoshop type *was*, and thus looked better. And if it looks better, it sells better.

This tendency to want to make pretty pictures of websites started causing problems; eventually I tired of explaining to clients after a site was built that they had been presented an impression and that the web was *just plain uglier than the mockups we made for them*. I turned off anti-aliasing and asked my employees to do the same. I didn't want clients to be unpleasantly surprised. For years, we had tried to be as realistic as we could in image editors like Illustrator and Photoshop. We paired this with the gifts of a) talking a lot and b) being able to explain vividly and accurately how things on the web would *really* look. Those tactics saved our butts on many projects. But those times are over.

The responsive web is the web as it was intended. It's not the desktop web. It's not the newest Safari browser web or the mobile web or the iOS web. It's not the tablet web. It's the universal web of information that should be universally accessible to everyone regardless of device or physical limitation.

Designing for the web is even more challenging now that we have what developer Jake Archibald calls *do stuff* sites in addition to *get stuff* sites. When designing *do stuff sites* (web applications), we need to think not only about form and content, but also about interaction. It is challenging to express this visually.

The specialist invasion

Long ago, many firms had just one person who did most of their web design. I don't mean things like project management and back-end programming. I mean visual design, interaction design, and often front-end development.

Front-end development around 1998 consisted mainly of HTML. There was also a lot of Flash going on. My first employees had no idea what CSS was; I had to explain it to them. There was still a lot we couldn't do with CSS. JavaScript—well, let's not even go there.

It certainly was possible for one person to design a website, mock up some pages in Photoshop, "slice" those Photoshop images up, and put them back together in HTML, allowing for the replacement of Photoshop-rendered text with the real thing, whether for small static brochure websites or as templates for a CMS.

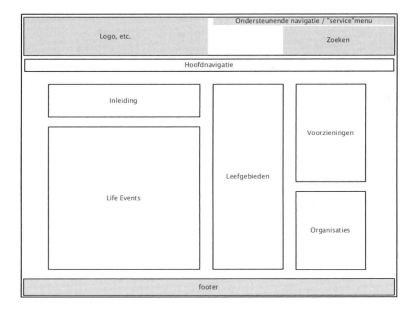

Figure 1.1
Early wireframes were often simpler than the wireframes commonly used today.

We used very simple drawings, then often called *wireframes* or *schematics*, to depict websites' underlying visual structure as we started thinking about them systematically and modularly (**Figure 1.1**). Even *get stuff* websites had *do stuff* aspects to them, and these things needed to be communicated during the design process.

We began to see a shift, in my experience around 2002, when projects were large enough and web work had become complex enough that we could start specializing in one or two specific aspects of the front-end experience. Many designers still wrote HTML, while site diagrams and wireframes were often the realm of the information architect. Tools like Jesse James Garrett's visual vocabulary gave us an abstracted way of communicating site structure and basic interaction simultaneously (**Figure 1.2**).[1] As interactions expanded from client-server interactions to smaller and more subtle interactions on the client side, specialists used increasingly detailed wireframes to demonstrate them. Wireframes began to look more and more like working web pages, only without color and imagery. Sometimes they were connected to one another to create prototypes with working links for clients to click through.

Before we knew it, something had happened: it became inefficient, though not impossible, to remain a generalist web designer. "Web design" had given

Figure 1.2
Many designers and information architects still use Jesse James Garrett's visual vocabulary to describe site structure and interaction.

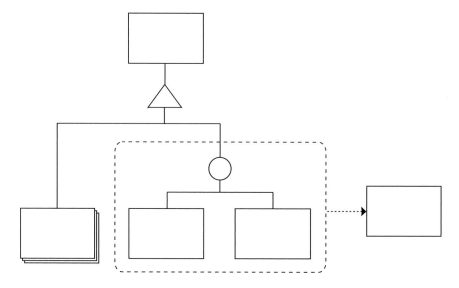

---

1 http://jjg.net/ia/visvocab/

birth to the specialist fields of information architecture, interaction design, visual design, and front-end development, happily followed years later by such fields as the desperately needed *content strategy* and the often ambiguous *user-experience design*. Wireframes, at this point one of the important deliverables of *interaction designers*, had become detailed enough that the role of the graphic/visual designer had changed slightly. In many web design and development firms, even at the time of this writing, visual design *follows* interaction design as part of the traditional **waterfall** process. This often means that designers are handed intricate wireframes that have been seen and approved by the client (**Figure 1.3**). As the client has seen and signed off on something that is quite detailed even in terms of page layout, it's often difficult or impossible for the visual designer to deviate from the basic design of the wireframes, effectively reducing the work of the visual designer to a color-by-numbers exercise. Visual designers are often required to base their work on these wireframes, changing typography and positioning things to an invisible grid, adding color and imagery, basically pouring decoration sauce onto the wireframe dish.

> In the **waterfall** model of website development, each step is done in isolation and the results of each step form the input for each subsequent step, similar to the way an assembly line works.

In this scenario, the *real* design work is done by interaction designers. They're the ones solving problems, while the visual designers are left to color within the lines. This hardly seems fair, as designers who don't solve problems are merely decorators. And decoration is not design.

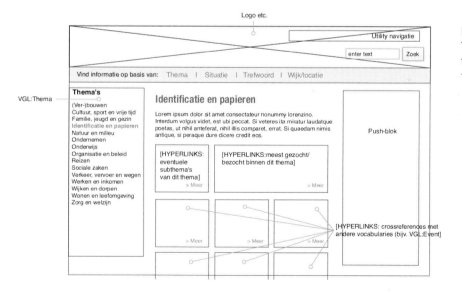

Figure 1.3
Today's detailed wireframes leave little to the imagination.

We're all interaction designers

Archibald's distinction between get stuff sites and do stuff sites isn't always clear-cut; sometimes even get stuff sites involve quite a bit of doing stuff. Searching or filtering information, logging in or requesting documents, filling out forms, even clicking through sections of the site are interactions that users do without thinking.

I'm of the opinion that the interaction designer and the visual designer should be the same person. In fact, I would assert that if you work on the design or development of the front-end web at all, you are in some way an interaction designer. There are aspects of what you do that can affect the experience (and thus the interaction) users have with your site or application. A developer who's concerned with optimizing performance is actively trying to improve user experience and interaction. A designer's purposeful use of color, space, size, and composition on a form is an attempt to make that interaction quick and easy for the user. The content strategist concerning herself with the importance of one type of content as opposed to another is thinking about improving the experience for the user.

This is not to say that "pure" interaction designers don't have their place. What I *am* saying is that graphic designers have been solving interaction, readability, usability, and aesthetic problems for centuries. There's no need to reduce them to decorators on the web. At the very least, interaction design, visual design, and content strategy (and perhaps other fields) should overlap much more than they often do today. This can be achieved by transforming each step in the design and development process from one that involves disciplines working in isolation to one that encourages collaboration during each step.

Jump from the waterfall

I propose leaving the waterfall method of web design workflow behind in favor of a multidisciplinary, iterative approach to design work for the web that allows clients to experience the evolution of a design from the very beginning with no opportunities for unpleasant surprises. I propose overlapping and combining disciplines, eliminating silos within the design process.

I support an evolutionary, iterative design process in which features and elements are added on an as-needed basis. This process is based on the principle of progressive enhancement: starting with nothing more than universally accessible structured content and working from that point forward to the desired complexity. This process starts small and grows. It's *messy*. No finishing wireframes first and handing them over to the designer. The wireframe is simple. The wireframe *becomes* the design. It evolves into it—*in the browser*.

The web affords us a wonderful opportunity: to be able to design and test a design in the actual medium for which we're designing. It's time to stop designing pictures of websites and start designing all aspects of the user experience simultaneously and in a practical way.

This book presents my attempt at creating such a process.

The straw that broke…

The thought process behind this book started about four years ago when I was working on a client project, creating my design in "Photoshop templates" as we called them: Photoshop documents representing web pages and the elements they contain. We needed depictions of quite a few pages to visualize the necessary elements. This was the normal way of doing things. However, in this case the company doing the front-end development required that every single element be exactly depicted in the Photoshop documents. If links were to be blue, *this needed to be consistent across all of the Photoshop documents*. We couldn't simply note the fact that links were such-and-such blue. The Photoshop documents *were the documentation*. Again, this was pretty much the norm at the time, but it didn't make me any happier when the client came back with feedback that some metadata needed to be placed between each paragraph and heading sizes needed to be changed. What followed was about two days of opening Photoshop documents, increasing their vertical size to accommodate the necessary changes, making changes that involved moving each bit by hand, and finally doing this across many Photoshop documents.

What in the name of all that is holy would have happened if that project was a "responsive" design project? After doing the same types of edits in about 100 different Photoshop documents (hypothetically 20 pages at five screen sizes), I would be curled in a fetal position in a corner of some dark place, that's what.

When I realized that two days of work could have been done with two lines of CSS, I decided at that moment that I would never make Photoshop "templates" again and I set out to create a new workflow that would save time and my sanity.

When I became an independent consultant in 2010, I had the opportunity to experiment with this workflow; clients had to accept my way of working as simply "how I work." I found that it worked well, not only for me but also for my clients. It wasn't without its problems (and still isn't). But compared to the waterfall method, it's quicker, easier, and more fun, and clients tend to like seeing the evolution of the design from structured content to finished design. They also seem to appreciate how much work goes into creating a web design. I don't have to tell them this; they *infer* it from the process.

The elephant in the room

One of the most important reasons to consider a new workflow is responsive web design. In its most stripped-down form, responsive web design makes a single, static representation of a screen or page absolutely meaningless. An image created in an image editor is not a depiction of a page in *any* browser, let alone in a variety of browsers within the context of an even larger variety of viewports on a variety of platforms (**Figure 1.4**). As far as I'm concerned, responsive web design has rendered these static representations obsolete.

Image editors remain a valuable tool—for *image editing* (surprise!), creating image assets, and creating exploratory images in the vein of mood boards or variations of them such as Samantha Warren's *Style Tiles*.[2] Photoshop and other image editors have become visual playgrounds for some. But as far as I'm concerned, the use of image editors for the creation of static mockups is officially old school, and I would encourage designers to put some of that creative energy to use exploring the medium for which they design.

---

2 http://styletil.es

This is not gospel

This is my process as it is today. It's messy in places. It's not a complete, A to Z procedure for designing and developing websites. It's visual design as I think it should be, with heavy overlap with content strategy, interaction design, usability, and *reality*.

The design workflow presented in this book has been used in real-life projects. It cannot be dismissed with a hand wave and a comment like, "That might work for freelancers, but not for our huge, *real* web projects." Indeed, this workflow has been used for large projects as well as small.

The ideas in this book are eclectic. Some are old, some are new, many are mash-ups of different ideas. You may find that your way of thinking aligns with some ideas better than others. The workflow set forth in this book is not right or wrong; it just might challenge some deep-seated thoughts and habits.

Figure 1.4
For layouts that change at different screen widths, static representations are time-consuming.

This is a challenge

This book will push you to think differently about how you design and what tools you use to do so. It will challenge you to learn some HTML and CSS if you don't know them already, as well as some commands in the dreaded command line interface. It will encourage you to look outside your own discipline for tools and thinking; you'll learn how some tools used by developers can free you up for more creative thinking instead of pixel-pushing, how to work more quickly and efficiently. You'll learn to actually *enjoy* it when clients make changes to your design. Well, to a degree.

This book documents almost two years of experimentation, observation, reading, thinking, and doing. This process works for me, but that doesn't mean it will work for you as it's described here. I invite you to find what works for you, your clients, and your team. My hope is that at least some of the thoughts in these pages will change the way you design for the web and the way you think about it.

Have fun, and keep learning.

2

FROM THE CONTENT OUT

"I know many, many people who would rather stab themselves in the eye with a pencil than be responsible for a large-scale content inventory. Me, I'm weird. I love 'em."

—KRISTINA HALVORSON

The first step in the responsive design workflow is to create a content inventory. Even if you're familiar with content inventories, allow me to explain how I approach the idea of structured content. You'll probably find that the content inventory I propose differs from what you're accustomed to.

It's often said that content is king. I tend to disagree. Designer Paul Rand described design as the "method of putting form and content together." Rand's statement confirms my opinion as a designer that content and form can either strengthen or damage one another. That said, *structured content can stand on its own*. Form (composition, color, imagery, and typography)—and the design that comes from combining it with content—can make information more accessible, understandable, and readable; it can make user interfaces feel easy to use.

Thus, I feel that design—as content and form combined—is king. *Structured content* is a very high-level official. This structure need not (and should not) be represented in a solely visual manner, but rather via metadata available in the medium in which it's presented: markup languages such as HTML or structural elements of a word processor, for example.

Structured content is semantic; it's about *what the individual pieces of content are*. This is a heading. This is a paragraph. This is a table cell that corresponds to a certain table heading. HTML, while not perfect, is now the primary way we structure our content on the web. We attempt to use the markup language semantically in order to describe what each element is. Where no element is available, we rely on HTML attributes such as `class`, de facto standards and conventions such as Microformats, or other metadata standards such as RDFa and Microdata.

Microstructure vs. modular structure

For the sake of naming things, let's say that text-level semantics compose a microstructure, as these tend to be the smallest elements of a web page. We can't break down text-level semantics much further, provided that structure has been accurately described. There are larger levels of content structuring possible. Let's take a login form as an example.

Figure 2.1
Even something as simple as a login form is built up from several basic HTML elements.

The login form in **Figure 2.1** is a structural element built from the smaller structural elements grouped within it. Some would call larger grouping elements *modules* or *components*. This form component consists of some basic HTML elements:

- A heading

- A label and input field for a username

- A label and input field for a password

- A checkbox for remembering the user's login data

- A button

- A link for registering and for retrieving a forgotten password

See what we've done here? The above list is a very simple content inventory. We'll come back to this later, but remember this example for when we do.

On a web page or on a screen within a web application, components are often built from smaller components or elements. For the purposes of this book, we're concerned with the components of a page, rather than the micro-structure of HTML building blocks that these components are made of. For example, we're more interested in the "main navigation" component than the `<li>` or other elements it's constructed from. We're more interested in the login form block than the input fields and buttons. We're primarily interested in components where elements are combined to work together as a whole (for example, the form elements combine to create a login form).

The lazy person's content inventory

NOTE

When I say "page,"
I also mean "screen,"
just in case you're
a web application
designer or devel-
oper who happens
to be allergic to the
word "page."

Jeff Veen has called content inventories "A Mind-Numbingly Detailed Odyssey Through Your Web Site."[1] Content inventories often list *existing content*. They're also usually exhaustive. We don't want that—it's way too much work. The first step in our responsive design workflow is to inventory *only the things that need to be on the page*, whether or not they exist yet. And by "inventory," I mean *make a simple list*. This version of the content inventory is not meant to replace traditional content inventories. We're simply borrowing the idea of a content inventory and using it as a starting point for design.

Remember the content inventory of the login form? This type of content inventory is the first step in the responsive design workflow: a simple list of the larger, meaningful components that need to be on the page. Think about the first page you'd normally want to visualize in an image editor like Photoshop. Think about the major content components you'd need on the page. That's the starting point for your list. Since there's a good chance you're not the person who'll decide which content goes where, it's a good idea to talk to that person before designing. Even though you'll just be creating design comps, you can only produce an appropriate design if you consider real content. Some of the necessary content may be listed on a traditional content inventory somewhere. If so, great! Try to use some of that actual content later in the design process.

Our universal example: This book's website

Throughout this book, we'll use a relatively simple example project to explain and illustrate each step in the responsive design workflow. The book's website (www.responsivedesignworkflow.com) contains everything you'll need for each step, and it's simple enough that the basic concepts won't be clouded by the size of the project. But don't let the simplicity fool you: I've used this

---

1   Jeffrey Veen, "Doing a Content Inventory (Or, A Mind-Numbingly Detailed Odyssey Through Your Web Site)". Adaptive Path. http://www.adaptivepath.com/ideas/doing-content-inventory.

same workflow successfully on large projects for large organizations. Once you've gone through all the steps, you'll start to see ways to implement the ideas on your own projects, both big and small. I encourage you to either walk through the creation of the book website, or if you prefer, to apply each step to a project of your own.

Every project starts with goals, with *reasons to be*. The book's website provides a specific and central place to promote the book, while offering various ways to purchase it. It also serves as a repository for errata and other news regarding availability, translations, and other useful information.

Progressive enhancement as design principle: The zero interface

Before we continue, I want to explain one of my governing design principles: the *zero interface*. I introduced this principle during a college lecture I gave several years ago and it became so integral to my thinking that I named my consultancy after it.

The zero interface is precisely what it implies: *no interface at all*. There's nothing between the user and the information that user wants, or the result the user is trying to achieve. The zero interface lets the user order something

ON THE SAME PAGE ABOUT PAGES

Of course, we're not designing individual pages. We're designing *systems*, frameworks within which pages will be constructed. So when I say "page," I'm referring specifically to the page(s) you would normally design in an application like Adobe Photoshop, a page *type*, such as a product page or a news article page. These are the pages you would show to a client during the design process. At this point, these are the only pages you need to worry about. Once the client gives the OK to continue in a certain design direction, there will be plenty of time to design the many different components you'll need.

from Amazon.com simply by thinking about ordering it. *Think, done.* I'd like that new book by David Sedaris. *Think, done.* I'd like everything I need to know about renewing my passport. *Think, done.*

Of course, this kind of user interface doesn't exist—yet. But that's not the point. When we design as if it does exist, it can help us make better choices.

The key thing to remember is this: *anything you add to the zero interface is perhaps one step too many.* It might exclude certain users or break your application on certain platforms. It might convolute the message or confuse your users. It might distract users from what they're trying to do.

If you use the zero interface as a design principle, you'll find yourself asking the same questions every time you're tempted to add an element to your site or app, whether it's a drop shadow, an entire section, or new functionality: Who needs this? Why do they need it? Are there more effective alternatives? Does it help reach the goals for this site? Since the ideal of "think, done" is not currently possible, what step or component is *absolutely necessary* for the user to accomplish her primary task?

For example, web designers often start by developing an idea for a general page layout. Navigation is one of the first things they draw in. But it's important to think critically: how do you know you need navigation? This is a shady example, since you'll *most often* need navigation. Base the choice on need rather than common practice. Take a footer, for instance. Do you *really* need one for your specific site? Get into the habit of thinking critically and challenging perceptions, even if—especially if—you're considering an often-used design pattern.

The reality is that as designers and front-end developers we don't often have the luxury of making these decisions on our own. Many of us are expected to just shut up and do the work we've been asked to do. This is unfortunate, but it's a fact of life we have to deal with. That doesn't mean you have to execute your work as a mindless drone. Anyone involved in the broader design process, from content strategists to visual designers to front-end developers, can think critically, and come up with more effective solutions to pitch to the decision makers.

NOTE

Websites are notorious for offering content that users don't need and lacking content that they do. This discussion is both outside the scope of this book and often not solely the designer's responsibility. If you want to read more on the subject, check out Indi Young's great book, *Mental Models: Aligning Design Strategy with Human Behavior* (Rosenfeld Media, 2008).

Creating the example content inventory

Remember that, for our purposes, a content inventory is just a list. It's a good idea to number each item on the list, so it'll be easier to refer to specific items later. Again, we're looking for essential functionality and content; we're thinking about content components as opposed to microstructure (HTML elements) or layout areas (header, footer, illustrious "main content," and "sidebar").

So what about the book website? In this case, it'll only be one page. This might change in the future, and if it does, then that will justify design changes as well. Regardless, the process of creating a content inventory remains the same.

Here's a preliminary list:

1. Title
2. Book synopsis/description
3. Purchase options and available formats
4. Errata
5. Publisher information

The goal is not to create an exhaustive inventory of the site's content, but simply to enumerate the content of *the page you're going to visualize.* You'll want to do this for each page you mock up. This example is the entire site, so that's killing two birds with one stone—you get the idea.

Since the inventory is just a list, you can make it in whatever format you prefer: a plain-text file, a spreadsheet, a mind map, or whatever fits your way of working. Then add a little more information about each item, similar to what you might find in a traditional content inventory. Note that in the following example, the descriptions are relevant to this particular website (and thus don't apply to *every* book website):

1. **Title**
   The title of the book won't be a logo, but the book's cover uses a specific font; the typographical treatment of the title should be consistent with that of the book.

2. **Book synopsis/description**
   This should include an image of the book and perhaps an image of a spread.

3. **Purchase options and available formats**
   You'll need to get more information from the publisher about this. For now, you can steal the basic format from other book sites by the same publisher. This will give you something to discuss and refine. (See "Instigating Discussion.")

4. **Errata**
   Obviously, this will be empty since this book contains no mistakes whatsoever. Well, one can hope, right?

5. **Publisher information**
   This could include contact information, but will it be enough to remain a separate element in this inventory? That's another one to discuss with the publisher.

Let's imagine that you discussed our little content inventory with the project editor and he gave you some feedback. First of all, he said it's quite common to include author information, such as a short bio and a photo. He also agreed with the single-page idea and that the purchase/format options would be the same as the publisher's other books, except for the price—which you can safely leave as a variable for now. However, he mentioned that since the book will contain code examples and various software is discussed, links to software and any necessary code should be included in the page. Also, it turns out that no extra section is needed for publisher information, since that will be part of the book description section.

This is valuable information, so you'll need to add it to the content inventory:

1. **Title**
   The title of the book won't be a logo, but the book's cover uses a specific font; the typographical treatment of the title should be consistent with that of the book.

2. **Book synopsis/description**
   This should include an image of the book and perhaps an image of a spread. It will also include publisher information, including ISBN numbers, number of pages, and so on.

INSTIGATING DISCUSSION

Sometimes, you'll have only a vague idea of what components will be needed for a mockup. This could be because you don't have enough information from the client, or because a very annoying project schedule has you designing before the content is finalized. Or it could be that the content is known, but you have some questions about it, like which bits are the most important. You could just throw some Lorem Ipsum in there (and Lorem Ipsum does have its place), but that would increase the chances that the mockup would differ significantly from the end result.[2] You have to know enough about the content to design with it.

When you don't know enough about the content of a page, you might try making it up or stealing bits from another source. I'm not suggesting you steal actual content from other sites; I mean using the same basic structure that other sites use. For example, for the book site, I've suggested in my notes that I don't know exactly what elements should be available in the purchase options and available formats section. By looking at similar websites, you can get an idea of possible elements and structure for this section. By adapting this reference content to the inventory, you accomplish two things:

1. You make it clear that you don't yet have enough information.

2. You create a discussion piece.

If the client (in this example, the publisher) sees the content inventory, she'll have the opportunity to provide you with the information you need. If that content or information is unavailable, then you might have enough to talk about and encourage the client to make a decision about the content in question.

If you have a content strategist on your project, he might be the one to provide you with the information you need or get it from the client for you. Always try to get as much real content or information about that content as you can. It will help you create a more appropriate, effective design and you'll save time in the long run.

---

2 Karen McGrane wrote an excellent little post in defense of Lorem Ipsum in certain situations: http://karenmcgrane.com/2010/01/10/in-defense-of-lorem-ipsum/

3. **Purchase options and available formats**

   The book will be available in at least one e-book format and as a printed paperback. Buttons or links will bring the user to the book page on a website (either the publisher's website or a website like Amazon.com) where the book can be purchased. A sample chapter will be available for download.

4. **Resources**

   This will include categorized—and when necessary, annotated—links to resources named in the book. Links can be to anything from articles to books. Any necessary code will also be available for download; demos will be linked to.

5. **Errata**

   Errata will be published for each reprint or new edition of the book sorted with the newest edition first.

This is detailed enough for right now. While it's important to design based on real content, it's important to remember that you'll be creating a mockup, not a website, so the smallest details can come later. There's no exact formula for determining what must be included at this stage. Generally, if you find yourself stuck because there are unanswered questions about content, then you need to get answers to those questions. But if you're obsessing about details that have little or no influence on your overall design, then you could probably prune your content inventory a bit, or put the details in the notes.

In the next chapter, we'll start creating responsive wireframes with the help of this content inventory.

Try it out

After reading through this chapter, you're probably seeing some problems with using this approach with your company or team. For example, as a visual designer, you might be handed wireframes from an interaction designer. You're not expected to think about (or question) content; that's already been set for you. This essentially demotes you to a color-by-numbers decorator, but what can you do? Well, if you're open to a new approach, go ahead and try creating a content inventory even if it's not expected of you. It's good prac-tice and will help you spot potential holes in the content, which you can then take to your team. Ideally, content strategists, interaction designers, visual designers, and even front-end developers should all be involved in the pro-cess of creating this content inventory. If there's one recurring theme in this book, it's that *we need to stop working in isolation*. Websites should not be built as automobiles on an assembly line. We need to accept that our disciplines overlap, and that we should *embrace this overlap and work together*. Whatever you can do to move your team in that direction will be all to the good.

At the basic level, content inventories are relatively easy to make. The first iteration should be done quickly, similar to a list of ideas in a brainstorming session. With each person thinking critically from his or her own expertise, the first iteration will probably be better than you think. In an ideal world, we'd have content strategists on every design or redesign project, doing the footwork on these inventories and persistently asking questions of clients in order to get the information we need.

Create an inventory only for pages that will be visualized in the form of a mockup. In other words, if you'd normally create a Photoshop comp of it, it's a candidate for a content inventory.

You can try it out now if you like. If you're a visual designer, think about any page you might be designing and create a simple content inventory following the process outlined in this chapter.

NOTE

When I refer to "Photoshop comp," I mean traditional static comps, regardless of the tool used, including comps made using Illustrator and InDesign.

If you're a developer and have received a Photoshop comp for a recent project, look at it critically and see if it all makes sense. See if you can reverse engineer a content inventory from what you see. If you're a designer, see if you can do the same with a wireframe you've been given. Try to identify the major content components of the page and analyze where the design or wireframe handles these well and where it doesn't.

If you're an interaction designer, you create the content inventory, adding interaction notes to each component, describing possible interactions and any other considerations for the designers and developers.

And leave your intricate wireframes at home, because old-school wireframes are back. And this time, they're pissed.

## 3

CONTENT REFERENCE WIREFRAMES

"A journey of a thousand li starts beneath one's feet."
—LAOZI, DAO DE JING

In the early days of web design, *wireframes*—sometimes called schematics— were simple drawings with boxes indicating where page components would go on the page. They were the precursors to mockups, a way to quickly try out content placement to get a feel for the general skeleton of the page. Nowadays, wireframes are often exceedingly detailed. They often contain actual content. Some actually look like almost-finished websites, devoid only of color, imagery, and typography. The layout is done. Decisions have been made about the content and the placement of this content.

At the risk of sounding like a grumpy old man saying, "Back in my day…," I find the current strain of intricate wireframes a very odd and limiting deliverable (**Figure 3.1**). The people who create them (often interaction designers) have done a lot of visual design thinking. Visual designers often receive these wireframes with a disclaimer that they're not intended to represent final designs. Yet this is exactly how some clients perceive them. I once had a client question whether I had sufficiently familiarized myself with the project materials because my visual design was so different from the wireframes made several months earlier. In the end, I was asked to use the wireframes as a basis for the layout. This sort of thing happens often enough that it's frustrating. Disclaimers of the "this is not the final design" variety are thus either untrue, or they render the entire deliverable useless. It doesn't represent the final design, but it might if the client really likes it. If the wireframe *does* represent the design, then it's a design, not a wireframe. If it doesn't, then why so much detail?

The problem with intricate wireframes, disclaimer or not, occurs *when clients see them*. If your wireframes are for team use only, disclaim them all you want. But as in the experience I noted above, when you show wireframes to a client,

Figure 3.1
Some wireframes look like finished pages, in some cases reducing the designer's job to a color-by-numbers exercise.

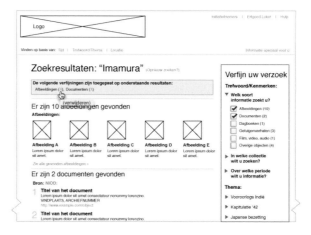

you're presenting a visualization; it's logical that the client might have expectations based on what they see. On the other hand, I've been involved on the flip side of the wireframe problem: more than once I've had clients and interaction designers actually negatively review my design proposals *because they looked too much like the wireframes.* How's that for a rock and a hard place? What if the interaction designer already came up with the best solution for something? So for some projects, designers are damned if they follow the wireframes too closely and damned if they don't. And that's damned frustrating.

Stop making this stuff so complicated

Detailed wireframes were presumably brought to life as a result of clients making fundamental changes when the design was already in the mockup stage. This is logical; changing a mockup can be an unholy amount of work. In fact, that's one of the primary reasons I changed my workflow and wrote this book. But creating a colorless, imageless "pre-mockup" in a different application is not the answer. The answer, as designer Mark Boulton says, is to stop going for *the big reveal.* Take your clients by the hand from the very beginning, and allow them to walk through your entire workflow with you. You won't need intricate wireframes. You just need to go back to using them the way they used to be: old-school wireframes.

I like to call those old-school wireframes *content reference wireframes* (**Figure 3.2**). I prefer that name because it describes how the wireframes deal

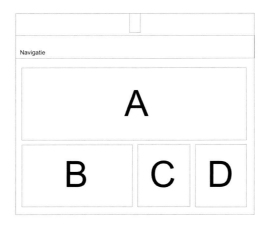

Figure 3.2
Content reference wireframes are minimal, referencing content rather than depicting it.

with content: they simply *refer* to it as opposed to *depicting* it. Every step in the responsive workflow is based on a simple idea; where step one involves making a simple list of content to be used, this step involves making simple wireframes that are nothing more than box drawings containing references to specific pieces of content.

What I propose in this book is that we stop heaping responsibility on the shoulders of wireframes. Let's use them to start visualizing content placement and relative importance in differing screen environments. Let's leave definitive layout and interaction design choices for later when we have a proper stage for them. In the workflow set forth in this book, low-fi wireframes will eventually evolve into hi-fi prototypes that can be studied, tested, revised, and client-approved.

NOW WAIT JUST A COTTON-PICKING MINUTE

Please note that my opinion on wireframes is based on my personal dislike of detailed wireframes and my questions about their usefulness in web projects. I have nothing against the interaction designers and others who make them. I have nothing against interaction design itself. I am, however, of the opinion that all front-end disciplines overlap with interaction design because most front-end decisions affect interaction with the site. Many of these decisions are made *after* the wireframes have been completed and approved. I also believe that studying and then modifying interaction can best be done in the browser through the use of a realistic prototype rather than a static wireframe. Here I don't mean clunky, clickable wireframes, but rather high-fidelity prototypes that are possible with the workflow described in this book.

Baby steps: Creating low-fi web-based wireframes

The first thing I'll ask you to do is to forget your pet application for creating wireframes, unless it's a text editor. We'll be using a text editor, HTML, CSS, and a browser to create our low-fi wireframes. Don't worry—it's easy.

For the book site, the content reference wireframe will be easy to make, not only because we're making just one instead of many, but also because we'll start with *structured content first*.[1]

At this point, we're just sketching an impression of the layout in the browser, so the linear layout is a great place to start.

Setting up your base markup

To start, you'll need a basic HTML document. I'm assuming you have some HTML knowledge and can divert from my examples and use your own boilerplates as you wish. If you don't have HTML experience, you might want to copy (or preferably, type) the code in my examples exactly.

Open your text editor and create a basic, boilerplate HTML document similar to this one:

```
<!DOCTYPE html>
<html lang="en">
    <head>
        <meta charset="utf-8">

        <title>Responsive Design Workflow</title>

    </head>
    <body>

    </body>
</html>
```

---

1 The idea of starting with structured content is similar to methodologies like Luke Wroblewski's *Mobile First*, where the visual lowest common denominator is the starting point. In this case, it's about starting with a basic content rather than a smaller screen size.

Next, look at your content inventory and prioritize the content. Consider a browsing environment where you'd be limited to viewing content in a linear fashion (and those environments are common enough). Which content is important enough to be at the top? What's not as important and should be underneath?

Another way of thinking about it is this: imagine that your job is to turn the content into a printed document, such as a book. Your content inventory suggests sections. Many of these sections will have a heading, and some of the sections might have subsections with headings of their own. How would you structure the content? What would come first? What would come last?

Let's take a look at the book site content inventory again:

1. Title

2. Book synopsis/description

3. Purchase options and available formats

4. Resources

5. Errata

This one is pretty simple. It seems logical and in the correct order in terms of priority. Let's go ahead with it.

Remember to work together. Linear content order is something that should be discussed among visual and graphic designers, content strategists, interaction designers, and clients, all of whom have valuable input or considerations to add to the discussion.

The next step is to create container elements in the HTML document that will represent the content from our inventory in the order we've determined. In the case of the book site, we'll place these elements in the body element:

TIP

Simple examples make things easy to learn. These techniques do work for complex projects. Throughout the book, think about how you could apply the various principles to your own projects.

```html
<body>
    <div id="page">
        <section id="book-title"></section>
        <section id="synopsis"></section>
        <section id="purchase"></section>
        <section id="resources"></section>
        <section id="errata"></section>
    </div>
</body>
```

The id attributes are optional, but as your wireframe evolves into a more detailed prototype, it makes reading your own code easier. Id attributes *identify* elements in your code, so this use—while optional—is totally appropriate.

With applications such as OmniGraffle and Photoshop, you'd have no HTML elements at all, so while some bit of HTML semantics is arguably better than none, your wireframe code becomes more important if you'll be using it as a basis for production later on. In that case, stick with your normal coding conventions (as long as they're good).

If you save your HTML document and open it in a web browser, you won't see anything, since we haven't added any textual content. Let's add some headings to the sections and number them, which will allow us to look at the page and see how the sections in the wireframe correspond to the content inventory:

NOTE

Classification in the document can be by class or ID. An ID is like a proper name and should be unique on the page. Thus, if you have reviews on your page, you might have a section with an ID of "reviews," with each review being another element (perhaps article) within that section with a class of "review." Many elements can share the same class.

```
<body>
    <div id="page">
        <section id="book-title">
         →<h1>1. Book title</h1></section>
        <section id="synopsis">
         →<h1>2. Synopsis/description</h1></section>
        <section id="purchase">
         →<h1>3. Purchase options and formats</h1></section>
        <section id="resources">
         →<h1>4. Resources</h1></section>
        <section id="errata">
         →<h1>5. Errata</h1></section>
    </div>
</body>
```

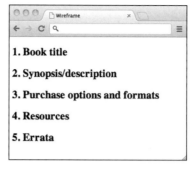

Figure 3.3
The section headings rendered with the browser's default styles.

Now when you view the document you'll see the content inventory displayed as HTML headings (**Figure 3.3**).

Next, we need to add some wireframe styles. To keep things clean, we'll add a special `class` attribute to the `body` element, which we'll remove later when the wireframe becomes a prototype:

```
<body class="wireframe">
```

This will ensure that the CSS rules you write for the wireframe won't be carried over into the prototype.

Setting up your base styles

Create a style sheet for styles that will almost always be used, regardless of viewport size. Call the document `base.css` and place it either in a folder with your HTML document or in a subfolder called "styles," "css," or whatever you prefer. If you're a developer, it's fine to stick with your own naming conventions, but be aware that the examples here assume there's a directory called "styles" in the same folder as your HTML file.

NOTE
If you prefer to use a CSS reset or normalize and are aware of the pros and cons, go right ahead.

Now open `base.css` in your text editor and give the `body` element a background color:

```
body {
    background-color: white;
    font-family: sans-serif;
}
```

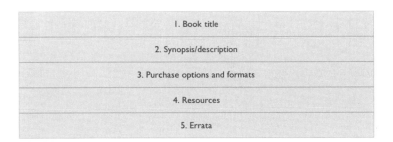

1. Book title

2. Synopsis/description

3. Purchase options and formats

4. Resources

5. Errata

Figure 3.4
The section headings with wireframe styles applied.

Next, add some style to the wireframe sections. These styles are purely for the purposes of your wireframes, so they mostly deal with how blocks are presented. You might choose a border, a background, or a combination of the two. Keep it simple! Here's an example (also see **Figure 3.4**), but feel free to create your own styles:

```
.wireframe section {
    background-color: whitesmoke;
    border: 1px solid gainsboro;
}
```

I'm using CSS color names here, but of course you can use any colors you please. These styles will be applied to sections only when the body element has the class *wireframe*, which is used only during the wireframe stage. This is the reason we set the font family: to make sure the wireframe styles don't conflict with any styles we'll add when the wireframe evolves into a full-blown design prototype.

To see how this looks in the browser, link to the style sheet from your HTML file:

```
<head>
    <meta charset="utf-8">

    <title>Responsive Design Workflow</title>
    <link rel="stylesheet" href="styles/base.css"
    ➝media="screen">

</head>
```

NOTE

I'm *namespacing* the wireframe styles in these examples by using the class "wireframe" on the body element. You could just as easily choose to have no class on the body and link to a separate wireframe.css style sheet, which you can remove when you move on to the design.

Now open the file in your browser. We're getting there, but there's a bit of tweaking to do. The headings are pretty large, dark, and flush left. I think centering the text in this case might make it slightly easier to read at a glance. Let's change that a bit:

```
.wireframe section {
    background-color: whitesmoke;
    border: 1px solid gainsboro;
    font: small sans-serif;
    text-align: center;
    color: silver;
}
.wireframe h1 {
    font-weight: 100;
}
```

The reason I'm using `small` for the font size instead of a specific unit (such as px or em) is that in cases like this where I simply want text to appear smaller, keywords like `small` are quick to use without even thinking about it. The key to making wireframes this way is to work as quickly as possible; detail is not yet important.

Next, let's add margins, and remove the default padding and margins on the body element:

```
.wireframe {
    margin: 0;
    padding: 0;
}
.wireframe section {
    margin: 1em;
    background-color: whitesmoke;
    border: 1px solid gainsboro;
    font: small sans-serif;
    text-align: center;
    color: silver;
}
```

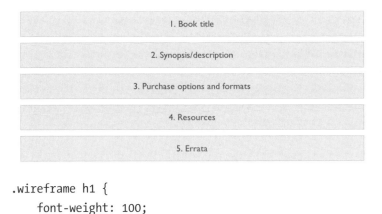

Figure 3.5
The section head-
ing with completed
wireframe styles.

```
.wireframe h1 {
    font-weight: 100;
}
```

This is looking reasonable (**Figure 3.5**). Depending on your own code, you may need to add or remove certain styles, such as adding some padding to the sections if you've chosen not to use borders.

This entire process of setting up wireframe base documents should take no more than a couple of minutes. After you've done it once, you can use the same setup for each project, which you'll then have up and running almost instantly.

Note that while I've walked through this step by step, it's very basic CSS and quite easy to do, even for beginners. You now have a linear, flexible-width wireframe that you can open and demonstrate in web browsers, even on mobile devices.

Adjusting the wireframe to be "mobile first"

If you can, either put your files on a web server and open the HTML page on a smartphone browser or use a mobile emulator. Whenever possible, try to test files on actual devices (yes, even wireframes). If you're unable to do one of the above, you can simply make your browser window smaller, but this is a poor substitute.

What you'll see is your wireframe in its current state: a listing of your content in a given order, and each content section displayed as a block on the page. The height of each block is determined by the size of the heading within it. This is not very realistic.

NOTE
Of course, resizing the browser window as a quick check to be sure that your style sheets are working properly is good practice so you can move quickly. But ideally, you should start check-ing all your files (even wireframes) on actual devices as soon as you can; it's a useful habit that can save you headaches down the road.

Focusing on how the wireframe looks in a linear fashion, as it will on many phones, try to estimate *roughly* how long you'll expect each section to be. *It doesn't matter at this point if your estimate is correct.* We know only that the defaults are *not* correct. So we estimate very roughly, and add some styles to the specific sections to reflect these estimates. We'll target the specific sections using their IDs, and continue namespacing with the *wireframe* class to avoid conflicts.

```
.wireframe #book-title { height: 5em; }
.wireframe #synopsis { height: 30em; }
.wireframe #purchase { height: 20em; }
.wireframe #resources { height: 50em; }
.wireframe #errata { height: 40em; }
```

An interactive way of adjusting these values is to use your browser's developer tools to adjust the CSS in the browser until you feel the height is about right, and then transfer that value into your style sheet (**Figure 3.6**).

Again, look at what happens in the browser. The values might be way off, but the feeling is somewhat more realistic, as the sections are not all the same size. Sections take up more space than headings alone, and these heights may vary significantly. Note that this process keeps moving back to the content. You're asking questions about the content and thinking about the content's effects on the page. If you're designing a web application (as opposed to a

Figure 3.6
Estimating the heights of content blocks helps you to quickly visualize what might happen with actual content.

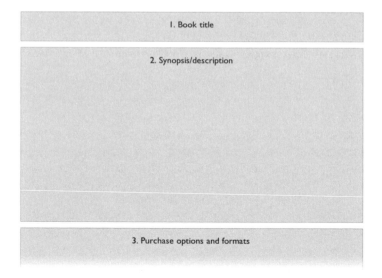

more informational web page such as our example), you'll already be thinking about things like the relative size of user interface (UI) elements and how much information you'll need to pack onto the screen. You might get some insight into future design choices such as a scrollable screen area versus multiple screens.

In fact, after the last changes you might have noticed the first problem our current wireframe has brought to light: in this linear format, we're forced to scroll down to get to any of the bottommost sections (such as buying the book). We've forgotten to add navigation!

Adding navigation

Navigation on small screens can be tough, with a lot of variables to consider. If we simply add navigation at the top of the page under the title or logo, that navigation might take up too much vertical space, in effect showing no more than menu items until the user scrolls down. Some developers solve this problem by collapsing the menu items with JavaScript, which works only if JavaScript is supported. My preferred method is to put the navigation at the bottom of the page and have a Menu link or button at the top of the page, which lets users jump down to the menu. This allows you to enhance the experience in environments where JavaScript is supported: the navigation is moved to the top and collapsed until the user clicks or taps the Menu link, which will show the menu items in a drop-down menu.

Thinking about navigation at this stage seems contrary to "keeping things simple," but it's good practice. You'll want to visualize how the navigation changes when the wireframe becomes responsive and is viewed at different screen widths.

Navigation involves interaction, and this is an opportunity for interaction designers, visual designers, and front-end developers to get together and think through the pros and cons of the different design options. This will also help later on if the client has questions about why certain choices were made. The moment when the completed wireframes are shown to the client is a wonderful time to start explaining (and demonstrating!) these considerations, that is, early in the design process.

Let's implement this bottom-of-page navigation pattern. If we decide later on that a different navigation model is necessary, we can change it fairly quickly, since the visualization in CSS takes only a few moments.

First, we'll add a section for navigation after the content sections:

```
<nav>
    <h1 id="nav">Navigation links</h1>
</nav>
```

Then add a link to enable jumping to that navigation. We'll put it above the sections, just within the "page" div:

```
<div id="page">
    <a href="#nav" class="menu">Menu</a>
    ...
</div>
```

We'll give the navigation the same styles as content sections:

```
.wireframe section,
.wireframe nav,
.wireframe .menu {
    background-color: whitesmoke;
    border: 1px solid gainsboro;
    font: small sans-serif;
    text-align: center;
    color: gray;
    margin: 1em;
}
```

Also, we'll add a rule to move the menu link to the top right of the page.

```
.wireframe .menu {
    position: absolute;
    top: 0;
    right: 0;
    background-color: gainsboro;
    padding: 0.5em;
}
```

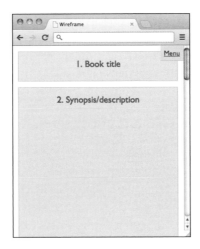

Figure 3.7 On small screens, it's common to provide a link at the top to jump to the navigation at the bottom of the page.

Now we have a linear wireframe with a link at the top right, which when clicked will bring us to the navigation block at end of the page (**Figure 3.7**). We can give this navigation block a height:

```
.wireframe nav { height: 10em; }
```

Again, we're just making a rough guess at this point. Although it's possible to do more complex things with small-screen layouts, please consider not skipping over the linear layout, as that's the default for users who get no layout at all.

A linear wireframe isn't all that interesting. While it did prompt us to think about things like linear content order and navigation, we haven't really had to start thinking about layout, which is something you'll normally do more of for larger screens. Now things get a bit more interesting: we're going to start wireframing this page for larger screens.

Creating variants for larger screen sizes

Imagine for the book site example that we want a layout that will work well on *most* smartphones and tablets, and in *most* desktop environments. We're not concerned with specifics yet; we want to start thinking about general layout issues, which we'll continue to refine throughout the design process.

What we're *not* going to do is look up sizes of specific devices. This may seem strange, but we're going to let the content dictate where our layout changes. Eventually, as we proceed, the points where these changes should occur (the *breakpoints*) will become clear (more on this in Chapter 6, "Breakpoint Graphs"). For the moment, we'll simply make some estimates, check the wireframes in a few devices, and adjust accordingly. This isn't an exact science. Sometimes, design is about what feels right.

The linear layout was just fine for small screens, now let's aim for the tablets. How big is that? Well, that varies. That's one reason why Ethan Marcotte stresses the importance of using a fluid layout grid when doing responsive design: device classes don't have set pixel-widths. They fall within ranges, and believe me when I say that those ranges will change constantly. So while I mention smartphones, tablets, and desktops specifically, don't take that too literally. You might be designing for TVs or portable game consoles. Designer Bryan Rieger recommends thinking in terms of *device classes* rather than specific devices. That's why you won't read anything in this book about how to get something to look a certain way on an iPhone or an Android device. The only

CSS MODULES FOR
SOURCE-ORDER INDEPENDENCE

In our example, the content sections are in the order in which they'll appear in the browser. The order in the code and on the rendered page is exactly the same (except for the Menu link). Two relatively new CSS layout modules will change the way we work with display order versus source order: Flexible Box Layout Module and Grid Layout Module. These will let you use CSS to display elements without regard to the order of the items in the source code. Each has strengths when it comes to layout. For example, "Flexbox," as it's commonly known, is more effective for laying out UI elements (think navigation, toolbars for apps, and so on), while Grid Layout is great for doing page layout. The two can be used in combination with one another, so you can lay out your page with Grid and certain components with Flexbox. Unfortunately, browser support for the newest versions of these specifications is very poor at the time of this writing, as they are still being actively developed. You can keep track of browser support by periodically checking the following links:

- http://caniuse.com/#feat=css-grid

- http://caniuse.com/#feat=flexbox

These pages also contain the links to the latest versions of the specifications.

way to know with any certainty how your layout will work on these devices is to test on them. Working with device classes is all about *inclusion*. We want to make sites and apps that are accessible to as many people with web-enabled devices as possible, regardless of device type or operating system.

There are actually two viewports we have to deal with on mobile devices: the visual viewport, which is basically the screen of the device, and the layout viewport, which is essentially equal to the width of the page being shown. (See the tip about PPK's two-part series on viewports for more on this.) For responsive design, we're interested in the width of the screen on smaller devices, and the *window* on devices and in browsers that support them. We need to tell the browser that when we say "min-width," the "width" of the page should be the width of the device (or the window). We do this by adding a meta element to the HTML (you can place it above the title element):

```
<meta name="viewport"
→content"width=device-width,initial-scale=1.0">
```

This both sets the width of the page to the width of the screen or window and sets the zoom to 100% (1.0), while allowing the user to zoom in if needed.

So our next step is to create a second style sheet for "tablet-ish" devices, with which we'll override some styles when the viewport reaches a certain width. Expand your browser window to the point where you feel the layout might need changing (this is still a bit of guesswork since we don't have actual content yet). Let's say that point is 600px. Use that as a starting point. Some tablet-ish devices will have larger viewports than that, and those might be better served by the desktop styles. That's the beauty of using device classes: it doesn't matter what the device is.

Create a new style sheet called medium.css and link to it from within the HTML.

```
<link rel="stylesheet" href="styles/medium.css"
→media="only screen and (min-width: 600px)">
```

Put this *beneath* the link to your first CSS file, so we can take advantage of the CSS cascade.

One thing we can immediately change—which is probably obvious—is the navigation. At 600px, it's likely we won't need to keep all the links at the bottom of the page. So we'll make some room for them and add them to the top

TIP

To learn more about viewports, especially on mobile devices, check out Peter-Paul Koch's A Tale of Two Viewports (http://www.quirksmode.org/mobile/viewports.html).

by adding a couple of rules to our new style sheet. These rules will override the rules in our first style sheet, only if our new style sheet is applied. We'll also hide the menu link:

```css
.wireframe #page {
    padding-top: 3.5em;
}
.wireframe .menu {
    display: none;
}
.wireframe nav {
    position: absolute;
    top: 0;
    width: 100%;
    height: auto;
    margin: 0;
    border: none;
}
```

Now if you open this page in a modern desktop browser and make the window narrow, you'll see the menu at the top right. Upon expanding the window, when it becomes 600px wide you'll see that link disappear and the navigation jump to the top. You can test this page in a few devices and tweak the media query as necessary.

My suspicion is that no other layout changes are necessary for this content at 600px, because it won't be wide enough to accommodate, for example, two columns of this particular content. But at about 900px, that's exactly what we're going to do.

Next, we'll create one more style sheet for our desktop styles and link to it in the HTML file:

```html
<link rel="stylesheet" href="css/base.css" media="screen">
<link rel="stylesheet" href="css/medium.css"
 →media="only screen and (min-width: 600px)">
<link rel="stylesheet" href="css/large.css"
 →media="only screen and (min-width: 900px)">
```

IMPLEMENTING MEDIA QUERIES

Media queries are pretty easy to understand. Let's take this one as an example:

```
<link rel="stylesheet" href="styles/medium.css"
→media="only screen and (min-width: 600px)">
```

The link element contains a media query. The only keyword ensures that the query will be interpreted only by browsers that understand media queries. Other than that, the media query says, "If the viewport is at least 600px wide, apply this style sheet."

I use a separate style sheet for each breakpoint in the examples in this book, but as with most of the methods I mention, there are always more ways to do things. In fact, there are four ways to use media queries with HTML documents. The two I most commonly use are:

1. Via the `<link>` element in the HTML (that's what I do in this book)

2. Using `@media` within your CSS:
    ```
    @media only screen and (min-width: 600px) { [your styles] }
    ```

3. Using it from within a `<style>` element in your HTML:
    ```
    <style media="only screen and (min-width: 600px)">
    →[ your styles ] </style>
    ```

4. Linking to a style sheet with `@import` (from within a style sheet)
    ```
    @import url(medium.css) only screen and (min-width: 600px);
    ```

I tend to use the first two methods, but often choose the first. You may use whichever you prefer. I personally like to use separate style sheets per break-point because it allows me to nest media queries; I can set a media query on a style sheet, and use `@media` within that style sheet as well. There are also some reasons not to do things this way, but these are only important for production code. Unless your code will be used in the actual site, simply choose one of the above methods.

I find the W3C's Media Query specification to be the best resource for learning more about media queries. And in contrast to some other CSS specifications, this one is pretty easy to understand: http://www.w3.org/TR/css3-mediaqueries/.

This third style sheet will be applied when the viewport width exceeds 900px. It's roughly at this point that we'll need to make some other layout changes. First of all, when we start dealing with actual content, we'll have to adjust the width of text columns for readability; that's something that should be repeatedly tested and adjusted. However, since we're not *yet* dealing with the rendering of actual content, we'll focus on layout changes. I think I'd like to have the book description and the purchase options side by side. I don't have to be sure, as visualizing this change is trivial. In `large.css` we can quickly try this out:

```css
.wireframe section {
    margin: 1em 0;
}
.wireframe #page {
    position: relative;
    width: 80%;
    margin: 0 auto;
}
.wireframe #synopsis {
    float: left;
    width: 58%;
    margin-top: 0;
}
.wireframe #purchase {
    float: right;
    width: 40%;
    height: 30em;
    margin-top: 0;
}
.wireframe #purchase+section {
    clear: both;
}
```

Hopefully, it's fairly clear what we're doing here, but for the sake of those less familiar with CSS, let's walk through it quickly:

◆ We remove the side margins on the sections because we're adding margins to the page by setting the width of the content to 80 percent of the viewport.

◆ #page is relatively positioned to create a new **positioning context** for the navigation.

◆ The synopsis and purchase information are floated left and right, respectively; height and margins are adjusted.

◆ The section following #purchase clears the floats. CSS trivia: I used an *adjacent sibling combinator* (the + sign) for this, so it applies to *any* section that immediately follows the purchase section. In this way, if we wanted to swap Resources with Errata we could do so without changing the CSS.

These changes result in a layout as depicted in **Figure 3.8**. You can test this first in a desktop browser by resizing the window (that's okay at this stage). If it's working, I encourage you to interact with the wireframe on various actual devices as well.

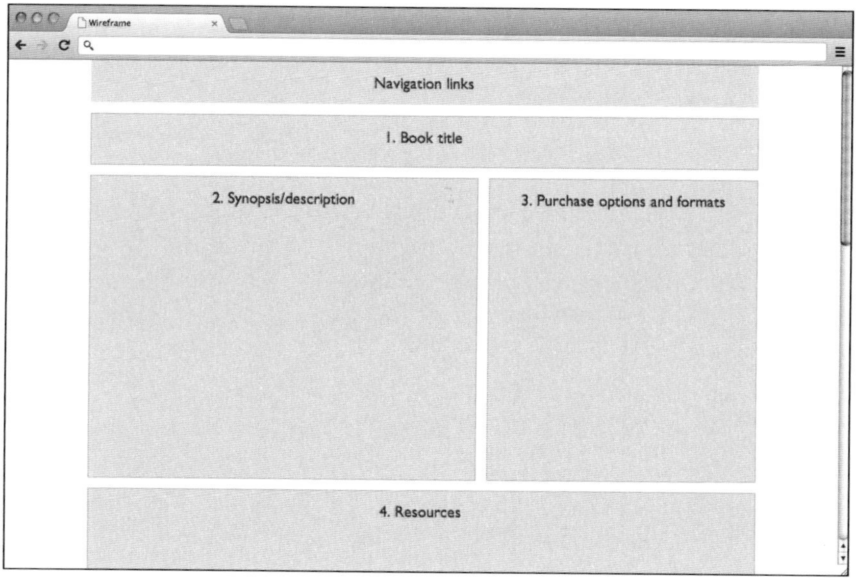

When we use `position: relative;` on #page, #page then becomes the **positioning context** for elements absolutely positioned within it. For these elements, `top: 10px; right: 10px;` would now refer to 10px from the top and right of #page.

Figure 3.8
In the wireframe phase, it's easy to play with layout ideas for varying screen widths.

Let's bust some myths

We're killing a couple of sacred cows here:

◆ The idea that interaction designers should make wireframes

◆ The idea that wireframes should contain detailed information about content

Some questions also arise:

◆ Does thinking about wireframes in this way limit design choices?

◆ Isn't it too early to think about layout?

◆ What should I wireframe?

◆ When do I involve the client (a.k.a. "Where's my fancy deliverable?")

Let's take a look at these to help alleviate some doubts, in case you're having them.

Interaction designers should make wireframes

I take issue with this. First, the role of the interaction designer is critical; he does not *need* a specific deliverable and should not be confined by it. On the contrary, good interaction designers are involved with *every* deliverable. Because most decisions affect interaction, the interaction designer should be involved throughout the design process. Since wireframes are exploratory studies of rough content placement, they involve design (layout), content strategy, *and* interaction, with a touch of front-end development expertise. All these disciplines can—and should—be involved in the process. You'll have to look within your team to decide who can best create the actual code. As you can see by looking at the HTML examples, the wireframes are created using elementary code that any web designer should be able to write in no time. It's the *thinking* about the content and other issues that requires time and discussion. And that's the most important part. Once that's done, these wireframes can be created very quickly. No ideas in them are set in stone.

How you approach this process depends on your team. You may sketch in a meeting and ask a front-end developer to work out the actual wireframe based on the resulting sketches. I recommend thinking about and creating the wireframes with the various disciplines in one sitting—and quickly. *Remember that you can quickly iterate if new insights on content or ideas arise.* Stop seeing wireframes as a polished client deliverable and start seeing them as a *tool for thinking* rather than the end result of thinking.

Wireframes should be detailed

No. Detailed wireframes involve too many design choices that are made in isolation from other important design choices. They introduce so many factors that discussions about them with clients can potentially spiral into design, content, *typography* (yes, it happens), and anything else under the sun, while still leaving a lot to speculation. I once had several members of a client team launch into a full-blown argument about one of the pieces of text—a single sentence—in a detailed wireframe. It's absolutely pointless. It overloads your clients with information in an attempt to get them to sign off on decisions that can only properly be considered when other factors, like the rest of the design and *actual* content, are at play. It's totally unfair to your clients and can result in changes at later stages of the project when everyone sees how things will actually be and are thus able to make sound decisions. Baby steps!

Do content reference wireframes limit design choices?

Absolutely not. The type of wireframe we've been playing with in this chapter gives a general indication of things like layout and navigation, but in fact it's about content order and priority. It's taking *nothing* and giving it a very simple form that can be built on. Since content reference wireframes are so quick to build, even drastic changes won't have much effect on your time or project schedule. They're best seen as sketches that will be fleshed out later. Content reference wireframes are 99.99 percent *less* limiting than the current popular brand of detailed—sometimes even "clickable"—wireframes that are designed to get sign-off from clients. It's very hard to deviate from something so detailed that's been seen and possibly approved by a client.

So, limiting? Nope.

Isn't it too early to think about layout?

Too early compared to what? We're not making definitive layout choices here. It's a sketch. We're *starting* to consider some things like layout. This kind of thinking, without going into too much detail, probably fits somewhere in between the thumbnail sketches and rough sketches graphic designers make. Sure, like many designers, I sketch on paper; these wireframes are a way to start transferring these types of sketches into the browser.

During the wireframe process, some valuable insights might make themselves apparent (like how I completely "forgot" navigation in our example). Most important, these wireframes inspire you to start thinking about *the shape of your content*, both literally and figuratively.

What should I wireframe?

You're free to wireframe as much as you want. I can only tell you what *I* do: I wireframe pages that represent *page types.* Websites are *systems* rather than collections of uniquely designed pages; most websites have a relatively small number of *page types*. When differences in content, goals, and functionality are big enough that the user interface or layout must change significantly, that's a new page type. Consider a registration page versus a product display; those are two different page types. If we see the anatomy of a web page as a combination of a *page type* and *components* (or *modules*), then wireframes are about page types. Most websites and apps don't have very many, even the largest websites. The most important pages are the ones people will use most often. These are the most-used screens in web apps and *content pages* in websites. Sure, you'll want to wireframe a home page because it's a different page type.

With *content reference wireframes*, wireframing anything more than the various page types is unnecessary. If you want to visualize more pages of the same type, you can do that when you create mockups. Later in this book, you'll see that *the wireframes will evolve into full-blown mockups.*

This workflow is designed to streamline the web design process, making some things quicker and easier to do while removing some unnecessary steps. Remember the 80/20 principle: 20 percent of the effort yields 80 percent of the result. Do as little as possible and stop feeling guilty about it.

When do I involve the client (a.k.a. "Where's my fancy deliverable?")

There's no fancy deliverable here. However, you should consider involving your client from the very beginning of this workflow and throughout all the steps. You won't necessarily ask for approval of these wireframes. They're not really that kind of deliverable. Feel free to ask the client's opinion, show the wireframes on different devices, and use them as a tool to prepare the client for how the web works and how responsive web design works. Content reference wireframes will get your *client* to think more about content in the same way they'll get *you* to think more about content.

Content reference wireframes are the second step in a cumulative and iterative design process. Iterations at each step are relatively small and painless; each step builds on the last, each giving a better glimpse into what the design will become.

Try it out

You might have (should have!) played around with the example wireframe we built up throughout this chapter. It was a deliberately simple example, designed to explain how I approach the process of creating content reference wireframes. As always, your job is to take the ideas that work for you and make them your own. You might want to style your wireframes differently. Your content is different than the content of the book website, so you'll likely have more page types and thus more wireframes to make.

Your estimates about the size of content will be different than mine. You might estimate your breakpoints differently. You might do many things differently, and that's just fine.

The important thing about these wireframes is to see them as quick, box-like sketches in the browser. Try creating a few wireframes for a project you're currently working on, just for fun. I'm sure you will find them fun and easy to make.

In the next chapter, we'll take some actual content and pour it into our wireframe. Another fun and easy step in the process, so get ready!

## 4

DESIGNING IN TEXT

"Plain text is the underlying content stream to which formatting can be applied. […] Plain text is public, standardized, and universally readable."

—THE UNICODE STANDARD, VERSION 6.1

Figure 4.1
The world's first web-
site was essentially
mobile ready.

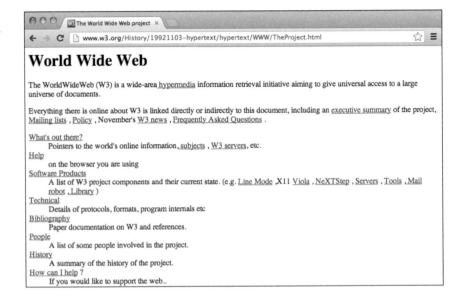

The world's first web page was practically mobile ready. And that was in a time when there were no tablets or smartphones. There's one simple reason for this: the web page consisted of *plain text*. Actually, it consisted of *structured text with hyperlinks*. This was how the web started, and the premise of structured content is still the basic foundation of the web (**Figure 4.1**).

We've added to the basic building blocks of the web, which were essentially (structured) plain text, hyperlinks, and images. We have technologies like JavaScript and SVG that let us draw on the screen, or even create entire user interfaces. Many developers advocate creating a distinction between web *apps* and web *documents*, referring to information-based websites, such as the W3C's first web page—or your blog—as web documents.

It's all content

We need not concern ourselves with the heated discussions about apps versus documents. For our purposes, if it's on the web, it's probably both. Most websites composed of documents are run by an application such as a content management system that requires a user interface. This tends to be the case even if the site's purpose is informational.

By the same token, I've never seen a web app without content. No app simply contains buttons with nothing on them, text fields without labels, and absolutely no text on the page.

One of the biggest problems in **web accessibility** is that many people start with the advanced user interface, take that as a given, and try to "add accessibility." Many websites are designed *from the UI in* rather than *from the content out*.

Take a geographical mapping application such as Open Street Maps or Google Maps as an example. It's easy for developers to plot out company locations on a map. When embedding these types of apps within a web page, there may be a focus on making that interface accessible—ensuring that the user can navigate with nothing more than a keyboard, for example. This is great, but there's a problem: technically complex or advanced user interfaces can't be viewed or used on every device. There's only one type of content that can be viewed on virtually any web-enabled device, and that is plain text, or rather, plain text that's been structured with HTML. Like it or not, HTML is the way we structure plain text for the web, because HTML is the single most portable and universally readable format at the time of this writing. Anything that can show websites can read and display HTML.

This means that there's an alternative approach to accessibility for complex interfaces, and for making any content universally available: start with the text-based foundation of the website or application you're designing, and then add the complex interface as a layer *on top* of this text base.

This might sound weird at first, but when you think about it, a mapping application *does* contain actual data and textual content. It's simply obscured from the user. We have to deal with a layer of abstraction to get to that information. Responsive design starts at the base: the structured content level. This allows sites and apps to respond to the user's environment, rather than expecting the user to respond to the interface (perhaps by grabbing a different device so she can actually use what we've built).

The way to do this is to start with the data, that is, the plain old textual content that's *always* available *somewhere*. Don't bury this under an avalanche of UI, but expose it from the very beginning. Allow that content to be the base on which you build.

So what about those company location maps? Well, the base data is probably a list of company location addresses, and perhaps other data such as phone

Web accessibility means that all people can access web content and services regardless of disability. It can also benefit those with technological limitations, such as an old browser or slow internet connection.

numbers and URLs. My opinion? Don't hide this data in a map. If you need or want a map, that's fine, but leave the textual data open for the user as well, instead of taking perfectly accessible data and hiding it from some users.

If you think this sounds a lot like progressive enhancement, you're absolutely right. That's what it is. And of course there are exceptions; there always are. But generally, many web apps are web forms at their core. Many websites are simply structured text at their core. By starting the design at the core, we can build websites that are more accessible and more usable by more and larger groups of people.

Starting design with plain text

Designer Bryan Rieger shares my love of plain text. During some correspondence with me about the subject, he shared these thoughts:

"One technique I've used for years is to 'design in text'… not necessarily describing everything in textual form […] essentially what is the message that needs to be communicated if I was only able to provide the user with unstyled HTML?"   —BRYAN RIEGER

Rieger's statement embodies most of what this book is all about: creating from the most basic, important content and working from that point forward. The technique of designing in text—that is, unstyled HTML—has some absolute benefits:

- ◆ As in content inventory and content reference wireframes, the focus is on content. In the case of designing in text, it's all about the *structure* of the textual content. Irrelevant content becomes easy to spot, as it's not hidden by the design.

◆ Designing in text utilizes one of the most important building blocks of the web: HTML.

◆ The **linear** form of structured text prepares us for the starting point for responsive design: the smallest screens with the least capabilities. (Remember the web's first page!)

◆ Clients familiar with word processors are probably familiar with the idea of linear, structured content (although some require an explanation of the difference between visual and structural formatting). It's relatively easy to convert word processor documents into structured plain text.

When I say **linear** here, I'm referring to content in a specific order, stacked from top to bottom, generally with the most important piece at the top.

When you create a page with unstyled HTML, you have created a web page that's mobile ready. From a *design* standpoint, it's also mobile first. With the default width of 100%, you might say it's on a single-column, flexible grid. This is a perfect starting point for responsive design.

Where content reference wireframes get us thinking about content at a block level, designing in text shifts the focus to the smaller bits of content. Let's take a look at how these ideas apply to the book website.

Marking up plain text

As Rieger pointed out, it's not enough to simply use plain text. We need to structure our textual content with HTML. There are several ways to do this, from writing the HTML by hand in a text editor to using a WYSIWYG editor. However, my preference is *plain text markup*, for which I use Markdown, although many other plain text markup languages exist.[1]

Plain text markup languages like Markdown let you write text in a very human-readable way (similar to how you would write in a text-based email program) and offer you tools to convert this human-readable format to HTML quickly and easily. Simple conventions denote structure. For example, a hash symbol (#) in Markdown denotes a level 1 heading. A word enclosed in asterisks (`*hello*`) denotes emphasis, in the same way you might use italics in a word processor.

---

1 To learn more about Markdown, check out:
   http://daringfireball.net/projects/markdown/
   http://en.wikipedia.org/wiki/Markdown
   http://en.wikipedia.org/wiki/Lightweight_markup_language
   (contains information about alternatives).

The best thing about using plain text markup is this: if your client or another party has created the content you'll use in your design, using a plain text markup syntax means all you have to do is copy the textual content, paste it into a text editor, and make use of the simple markup conventions. This is much simpler than, say, turning the text into HTML by hand.

The book page text in Markdown

The following is some text we'll use for the book site design. This is the minimum amount of content I'd like to use to communicate with visitors to the page. Save the following text (or your own example text) to your project folder and call it whatever you please. Since it represents the content of a home page, I'm calling it `index.markdown`.

THE TOOL RULE

In this book, there's a lot of talk about process, and there's a lot of talk about tools. Let's agree on the Tool Rule: it's not about the tools. The process is most important.

I need to use tools to demonstrate the workflow laid out in this book, and the best way to do that is to demonstrate using the tools I use in real projects when incorporating this workflow. This doesn't mean that the tools are right for you. Admittedly, some are quite geeky, and where I use a command line program, you might prefer a graphical equivalent. That's okay. Just remember that for all the talk of tools in this book, the specific tools used here are not essential for putting the responsive design workflow into practice. You'll work most effectively when using tools you're familiar and comfortable with.

That said, if you don't already have appropriate tools for any of the steps in this workflow, why not try out the ones mentioned in the book? If you're a designer, don't be afraid of text-based tools or the command line. You might be pleasantly surprised at how quick, effective, and fun they can be!

So if you prefer Textile or reStructuredText to Markdown, it's fine to stick with them. If you prefer you own home-brewed Markdown converter to Pandoc, more power to you. (You're missing out, though!)

You get the idea. Whenever I use a specific tool in this book, remember the Tool Rule and use a tool that you're comfortable with, as long as it helps you get the job done. Tools are the means, not the end.

Responsive Design Workflow

by Stephen Hay

In our industry, everything changes quickly, usually for the better. We have more and better tools for creating websites and applications that work across multiple platforms. Oddly enough, design workflow hasn't changed much, and what has changed is often for worse. Through the years, increasing focus on bloated client deliverables has hurt both content and design, often reducing these disciplines to fill-in-the-blank and color-by-numbers exercises, respectively. Old-school workflow is simply not effective on our multiplatform web.

Responsive Design Workflow explores:

- A content-based approach to design workflow that's grounded in our multiplatform reality, not fixed-width Photoshop comps and overproduced wireframes.
- How to avoid being surprised by the realities of multiplatform websites when practicing responsive web design.
- How to better manage client expectations and development requirements.
- A practical approach for designing in the browser.
- A method of design documentation that will prove more useful than static Photoshop comps.

Purchase the book

Responsive Design Workflow is available in paperback or as an e-book. The book is available now and can be ordered through one of the booksellers below.

```
- [Order from Amazon.com]
- [Order from Peachpit Press]
- [Order from Barnes & Noble]

## Resources

[Lists of resources per chapter?]

## Errata

[Lists of errata per chapter?]
```

Now this is interesting. In previous chapters, we discussed how problems can arise from insufficient thinking about how content will actually work—think back to the example where I "forgot" that we might need some sort of navigation. This may seem an unlikely example, but we've all experienced situations where we realize that things have been omitted or not thought through. Working in small steps *from the content out* can expose issues and avoid these problems. This Markdown document exposes a flaw in my thinking about resources and errata that becomes clear when we start designing the page in text. If I have both resources and errata for some of the same chapters, I'll get something like this:

```
## Resources

* [Chapter 1](http://www.example.com/resources/chapter1)
* [Chapter 2](http://www.example.com/resources/chapter2)
* [Chapter 3](http://www.example.com/resources/chapter3)

## Errata

* [Chapter 1](http://www.example.com/errata/chapter1)
* [Chapter 2](http://www.example.com/errata/chapter2)
* [Chapter 3](http://www.example.com/errata/chapter3)
```

Although this won't get us arrested, it's redundant. It makes more sense to have a page for each chapter, and having anything relevant to a given chapter on that particular chapter's page. This means that I'm going to change my mind at this point in the process (clients tend to do that, as you probably know).

Keep in mind that any mind-changing going on at this point is not only *not a problem*, it's also *a good thing*. Better to make content-related and structural changes now.

Instead of Resources and Errata, I want a list of chapters, with each item being a link to that particular chapter's page, which can contain sections for Resources and Errata. Come to think of it, we'll need to put up code samples as well, so the chapter pages are a great place to put those.

What changes mean at this point

Changes at this point in the process entail relatively non-labor-intensive edits to one or more of three things: the content inventory, the content reference wireframes, and the structured text design (that is, your Markdown document).

Of course, since our example is currently one page, changing these is simple. Remember that most websites, no matter how big, are a combination of user interfaces for interaction and containers for content that's poured in from a database. The focus of the first three steps in this workflow is these larger entities: *types* of pages, *types* of user interfaces, and *types* of content. While you're free to use these steps to design individual pages, you probably won't want to do that for the individual articles in a site like nytimes.com.

Think in terms of types. Think in terms of components. There are never many page types, so don't think too much about *pages*. One of my most challenging conversations with a client involved me explaining that I didn't have to redesign their site's 10,000 pages. Rather, we had to spend a lot of time analyzing their content, and then I would design about 10 or 12 pages (plus a battery of small components). I would be designing a *system*. Not individual pages.

The change I've made to the book page means there's another page type, since the *content of that page type dictates that it should be different than the home page.* That last point is important. There's been a lot written about designing the user interface first. I agree in most cases, but not all. The user interface serves a purpose and contains content relevant to that purpose.

TIP

It's easy to forget that clients don't always think the way we do. We're influenced by our experience with technology and the heavy use of abstraction in modern web work. Be patient with clients and explain things in plain language, like a chef giving a tour of his kitchen to a guest.

Both purpose and content are the foundation of the interface. And that thinking is also part of the whole design process.

Before we make the changes to our example, let's think about what these changes mean for us while utilizing the responsive workflow:

1. We need to create a content inventory for the second page type and change the existing one accordingly. This would have to be done within any workflow that involves content inventories, not just the workflow described in this book.

2. We need to create a new wireframe and modify the existing one. In plain English: we need to remove one box from our existing wireframe and create another HTML page with a few boxes on it. Oh, the pain.

3. We need to change the last section of the Markdown document and create an additional one. Since we don't actually have resources or errata yet, we'll have to define the "shape" of that content by coming up with a real-world example we can test and discuss with the client.

These steps are not difficult. If you're a graphic or visual designer, you may not find it exciting. In fact, someone else can do these steps. But that person is absolutely part of design, and as I mentioned previously, all parties should be involved. Yes, the client, too—*especially* the client. You'll reap the benefits later.

Now, contrast this with the waterfall process. In the traditional workflow, there is no designing in text step. The wireframes are detailed and intricate. The content inventory may or may not exist. So the problems with changes start with wireframes. Sure, we need to change the text in the Markdown document, much as we'd change text in a complex wireframe. But the main difference is that when designing in text, *the changes we make are text-based*. Detailed wireframes contain text, but this text is still presented in a highly visual form in relation to other elements on the page. There may be no color, but there is typography. There is layout, to a certain extent. By contrast, plain text markup is all the same font and denotes only textual structure. Changes in a Markdown document don't require typographical changes or changes in layout. New pages don't require a new layout. We're not at that point in our process yet, so changes are much easier to make.

Content reference wireframes are also very easy to change. After all, they're just boxes, aren't they? They become more important down the line, but for now, we're compartmentalizing changes. Content changes should be content changes, not content-typography-layout changes.

This approach allows us to "help" the content. In return, content will help us down the line. Because we've given it the attention it deserves, it will help us with layout, with determining breakpoints, and with many other aspects of the design. There are always cases where huge changes to a project will come during the final stages of design, and this process is designed to minimize the chance of those changes occurring—and minimizing the impact of those changes if they *do* occur.

It's about thinking

Again, the book page is a very simple example, but this could just as easily have been a sign-up page for a product or service (or any other page or component), where designing in text might help you make better decisions. As with content inventory and content reference wireframes, designing in text gives you an opportunity to change things before doing so endangers the schedule or results in high costs.

We're designing in text here simply by putting text down in a Markdown document. That fact should make it clear that the process of designing in text is not about Markdown; it's about thinking. It's (as in the first two steps) about content and its structure.

Personally, this is one of my favorite steps in the workflow. The beauty is not only in its simplicity, but also in the fact that once you convert this document into HTML, you have a mobile-ready mockup of a web page in structured text that you can load into virtually any browser that parses HTML. This is a *huge* advantage.

Converting plain text to HTML

Practically every plain text markup language has a way to convert structured text into HTML. In fact, Markdown might be one of the most complex, because there are so many different versions of Markdown itself. (These versions are often called *flavors*. Don't ask me why—hungry techies, perhaps.)

The original Markdown lacks an equivalent for every single element available in HTML. This is actually a strong point: it contains equivalents for the most commonly used text elements, and lets you use plain HTML when needed. In that sense, Markdown is not a language of its own; it's a *front end* for HTML.

TIP

Remember the Tool Rule. If Markdown isn't your thing, or you're just interested in exploring some other options, see http://en.wikipedia. org/wiki/Lightweight_ markup_language for an overview of similar markup languages.

This means that if you want tables, you can enter them in HTML and that's a totally legal Markdown document.

But this makes Markdown just that much more difficult for nontechnical people (perhaps even your clients) who'll be preparing the documents for this step in the workflow. As I was developing this particular workflow, I toyed with the idea of using a more "complete" text markup language, but I was already so familiar with Markdown from use in email and other applications that I wasn't too keen on switching. Luckily for me, as I mentioned, there are several different **implementations** of Markdown.[2]

Some of the Markdown **implementations** are simply conversion tools, allowing one to convert Markdown into HTML or vice versa. Others are both conversion tools and extensions of Markdown itself, adding the ability to denote an expanded set of elements in plain text, such as tables and more.

I chose an implementation called Pandoc.[3] Pandoc supports the original Markdown and offers extremely useful optional extensions, such as definition lists, numbered example lists, tables, and more. Pandoc can convert to and from a bunch of file formats, which is wonderful and has so many uses beyond web design workflow.

This will be the first of several instances in this workflow when you'll be typing things into the command line. In case you're not familiar with the command line, you'll most likely be using the Terminal application on OS X or Cygwin on Windows. If you use Linux, there's a good chance you've already used your terminal application at some point.

Using the command line

The command line interface (CLI) provides a simple means of interacting with your computer. Its design is actually quite elegant: on the screen there's a *prompt*, at which you can tell the computer what you want it to do, and it will do what you ask (**Figure 4.2**). If it doesn't understand your command, it will tell you so.

People like to bring up the potential drawbacks of the CLI: yes, there are commands that will erase your entire hard disk or a portion thereof. Just *don't type those commands*. In the graphical interface of your computer you wouldn't willingly select all your folders, move them to the trash, and then empty the trash.

---

2 http://en.wikipedia.org/wiki/List_of_Markdown_implementations

3 http://johnmacfarlane.net/pandoc/ If you're interested in Pandoc, you can try it before installing it at http://johnmacfarlane.net/pandoc/try.

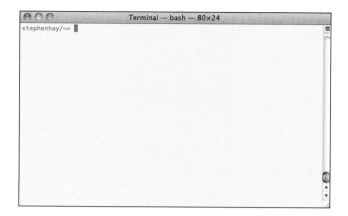

Figure 4.2
The command line
interface is sparse;
you have to tell it
what to do.

The argument is that it's easier to do something stupid like that in the command line. And arguably it is. In fact, many things are easier to do in the command line, not just stupid things. Commands aren't difficult, though some of them can be difficult to remember. But practice helps with memorization, just as it does when you need to remember which submenu item to choose in a graphical interface.

So don't be afraid. The command line is a very useful tool, just as graphical applications can be. And as with any computer interface, you need to think about what you're doing. Just remember that the command line does what you tell it to, nothing more, nothing less. Don't tell it to do stupid things and it won't.

The beauty of the command line is that you don't need to know everything about it. It helps to know some basic commands—such as those allowing you to navigate around your system and create, copy, move, and delete files and folders—but mostly what you'll need to know are the commands specific to the software you're using.

If you're skeptical, consider Adobe Photoshop (**Figure 4.3**). Photoshop—which this workflow deems unnecessary for creating design mockups for the web—is one of the most complex and sophisticated pieces of software available to consumers today. There are hundreds of books on how to use Photoshop, as well as whole books that cover only a specific functionality. If you're a designer, you've most likely used Photoshop. So there you are, proficient in this really advanced piece of software, but worried about the command line. Believe me, you are absolutely smart enough to learn commands in the command line. And someday when you discover more command line tools and are able to do things like resize fifty images in about three seconds,

NOTE
I'm making the assumption that you either have a terminal application or are capable of installing one. Linux and OS X have terminals built in. Windows users can install Cygwin from www.cygwin.com.

Figure 4.3
Graphical interfaces like Photoshop's provide buttons and other inputs to let you tell it what to do. While visual, they're not necessarily simpler than the command line.

you'll feel the power that your developer friends do. If you're a developer and reading this, yes, go ahead and gloat.

I recommend that you consult a resource like Zed Shaw's CLI Crash Course to become familiar with the command line. The online version is free, easy to follow, and you really will learn all the basics.[4]

That said, there are few commands you should know now: *pwd*, *cd*, and *ls*. Go on, open up your terminal application. This puts you in a *shell*. On OS X, the system I currently work with, the standard shell is called *Bash*.[5]

As a web worker, you've very likely *seen* a terminal before, but if you're not familiar, that little blurb of text you see to the left of the cursor is called a *prompt*. It's customizable, and it tends to look different depending on both the system and the user. It may or may not tell you information about the system or the folder you're in. No matter. You type commands at the point where the cursor is. Type one now: pwd. You'll see something like this:

```
$ pwd
```

Now press the Return key. The CLI returns a *path*. Just like paths on a web server, this is a path of folders on your computer. The path you see leads from the root folder of your computer to the folder you're currently in. pwd means

NOTE
Throughout this book, the command line prompt is denoted with a dollar sign ($). It represents your own prompt; you should not type it in as part of the command.

---

4 http://cli.learncodethehardway.org

5 *Bash* stands for "Bourne-again shell". See http://en.wikipedia.org/wiki/Bash_(Unix_shell)

print working directory. The command tells the computer to print the working directory, which is the folder you're currently working in. This is useful because, in contrast to your system's graphical interface, you don't always have a visual clue of where you are when you're in the command line. This is what I get when I execute pwd:

```
$ pwd
/Users/stephenhay
$
```

Yours will be different, unless your name is Stephen Hay (in which case, nice name!). No problem; now you know where you are. Let's see what's in this folder. We can *list* the files in the current folder with ls:

```
$ ls
Applications   Documents   Library     Movies
Pictures       Desktop     Downloads   Mail
Music          Public
$
```

Your results might be shown differently, depending on how many files you have and the width of your terminal window.

You'll also want to *change* your *directory*, which you can do with cd:

```
$ cd Applications
$
```

This puts me in the Applications folder. You might not have the same folder; just enter the same command in one of your own folders.

My own prompt contains information about where I am (it actually contains the name of the folder I'm in), but I've customized it to do so. You needn't worry about that at this point. As you become more comfortable with the command line, you can learn how to customize your environment.[6]

---

6 Many years ago I learned how to customize my own prompt by reading Daniel Robbins's easy-to-understand article on the subject, which can be found at http://www.ibm.com/developerworks/linux/library/l-tip-prompt/.

So moving down is easy: just type `ls`, note the directory you'd like to move to, and `cd` to that directory. Also note that many shells let you use the tab key for completion. This means that instead of typing the full word `Applications` in the previous example, I could type an `A` or `Ap` followed by the Tab key, which would complete the word for me. When the completion matches several words, these will be shown and you'll need to add one or more letters accordingly before pressing Tab again. This is a huge time-saver:

```
$ cd A [press Tab key]
$ cd Applications [press Return key]
$
```

Now you know how to move down a directory. Moving up is easier. A single dot is the symbol for the current directory, and two dots is the symbol for the parent directory. Moving up a directory is done thus:

```
$ cd ..
```

followed by pressing the Return key. Moving up two directories would entail:

```
$ cd ../..
```

and so forth.

That's enough to get you started. If you have no previous CLI experience, try these commands out for a while. You can't do anything bad to your system, because these commands don't alter anything.

Converting to HTML

The first step in using a command line tool—unless it comes with your system—is to install it. I'm assuming Pandoc doesn't come with your system, so you'll need to install it if you're planning to follow along in the book. On Linux, you might find it and be able install it via your package manager. For OS X or Windows, there are install packages available.[7] Go ahead and install Pandoc (or your preferred plain text converter) and then come back.

---

7 http://johnmacfarlane.net/pandoc/installing.html

Once you've installed Pandoc, use `cd` to navigate to the folder that contains your Markdown document. Then type the following command:

```
$ pandoc index.markdown -o index.html
```

This says, "run Pandoc on the file `index.markdown`, convert it to HTML, and save the output of this command as `index.html`." If you run `ls`, you should see that `index.html` has been created (**Figure 4.4**). Open this file in a web browser. Your structured content is now HTML. And it works on practically every device.

It just doesn't look very pretty yet, so let's do something about that. In the following chapter, we'll start thinking about the more visual aspects of the design process, using this content as a base.

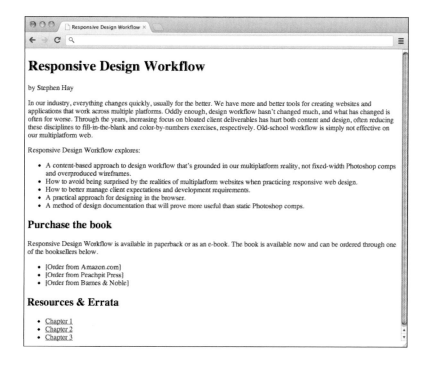

Figure 4.4
Using a command line tool like Pandoc, it takes only a second to turn plain-text markup into a basic HTML page. This can be a huge time-saver.

## 5

LINEAR DESIGN

"It's pretty simple.
On a phone,
full-size websites suck."
—PAUL CAMPBELL

On most small viewports—such as those on phones—we can only view the content of a web page in a linear fashion. It's possible to place things side-by-side on many devices, but not all of them. It depends on both the size of the device and the level of CSS support. In this chapter, we'll look at determining breakpoints for our design and content based on device classes and what the content and design do at certain screen widths.

NOTE

When I speak of *linear design*, I mean the design of linear content. Color, type, and images may be used, but the design has no layout other than that the content is stacked vertically.

First, though, we need to accept the fact that the lowest common denominator of devices will allow us to view only structured text content, similar to what we produced by converting our Markdown documents to HTML. The earliest web-enabled phones should be able to handle this content, even though it's not pretty—the text will display even where CSS support is absent. Text browsers also fit into this device class. One step above these are devices on which CSS *is* supported. We'll still use the structured text content, but CSS lets us apply some visual aspects to the design. Because CSS support varies from device to device, our approach should be like a layer cake. Even at this level, progressive enhancement is important.

A **reference design** could be a single image or sketch that inspires the design at every screen size. It could also be several sketches, for example, one at roughly 320px, one at 600px, and one at 900px, each approximating how the site should look when close to a given width.

Developing a design language

Bryan Rieger has written about the importance of a **reference design**.[1] A reference design is the design of a website or app at one or more strategically chosen sizes based on carefully chosen device groups. You can look to these when creating a responsive design, without having to design for every single screen width. This is where the process gets personal. Many people will want to create a desktop design and then make the linear design a derivative of that. You're free to do so, but it defeats the purpose of this workflow. I recommend a process that takes us incrementally and cumulatively from the smallest and simplest aspect of our design to the largest and most complex variable.

So while the approach Rieger outlined a few years ago is still sound and you can use it effectively today, I'm going to challenge you to start designing your content without yet *fully* knowing what your "desktop" version will look like. This takes the idea of *mobile* first pretty seriously from a design standpoint, and will absolutely feel like walking around in the dark.

We'll be using a variation of Rieger's process where the design of the content within a linear presentation is the reference design. Scary, right?

---

1 http://mobiforge.com/designing/story/effective-design-multiple-screen-sizes

Even though the workflow described in this book makes changing things less of a problem than in a waterfall workflow, we still need to be careful. We have to *consider* other screen widths and browser environments, even though we're postponing their design. We can do this by developing a *design language*. Graphic designers will probably know what I mean by this. For the more technology-driven reader: a design language is like any other language— it gives you the building blocks to create practically anything you want.

I tend to think of visual language as consisting of four components (listed here in no particular order):

◆ Layout (general usage and composition of space and elements)

◆ Color

◆ Typography

◆ Imagery (whether photography or illustration)

Some designers will disagree, citing more components or fewer. That's fine. I think in terms of these four, and I'll use these in my examples.

Using the Design Funnel

Seldom can a designer make arbitrary choices regarding the components of design language, haphazardly injecting fonts and colors without starting from some kind of base. Spontaneity may be desirable in art, but it's usually not in design. Design solves a problem. So what problem are you trying to solve?

The *Design Funnel*, my pet name for the process I follow to create the design language, involves the things designers do that can't be seen (**Figure 5.1**).[2] It moves the vague client exclamations about goals and values ("we're *professional, trustworthy,* and we want a *dynamic* website") through an imaginary funnel that turns them into a concrete design language. It's not a new method, but it's surprising how many designers skip the crucial first steps. They jump into creating a design and extract the design language from the design after the fact. That's a horribly ineffective way to work (though I've also been guilty of it, so I'll be the last to judge).

The Design Funnel distills what you've learned from your client into a tangible language you can use to create your designs.

2 http://changethis.com/manifesto/show/48.04.DesignFunnel

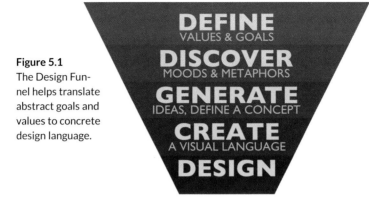

Figure 5.1
The Design Funnel helps translate abstract goals and values to concrete design language.

A GREAT EXAMPLE OF DESIGN LANGUAGE: MAILCHIMP

For the skeptical: think about MailChimp,the email newsletter software with a personality.[3] That personality find its way into the design of the website and application by way of design language (**Figure 5.2**). Of course, we're referring to visual design, but all aspects of MailChimp align with the goals and values of the company, including things like usability and content as well as visual design. The entire user experience is immersed in this personality.[4]

I'm not saying the designers at MailChimp used the Design Funnel, but they did go through a similar process: they translated goals and values into tangible things using a fun tone of voice, cute illustrations, and a pleasant color palette. The typography supports maximum clarity and readability. I'd lay odds that even the choice of rounded corners was for consistency with the MailChimp personality. Really, that's the only legitimate reason to make a design choice: to help achieve a goal, solve a problem, or tell a story.

---

3 http://mailchimp.com

4 Aaron Walter describes in detail his thoughts on making the human connection in design in his book *Designing for Emotion*, in which he also discusses the MailChimp design (http://www.abookapart.com/products/designing-for-emotion).

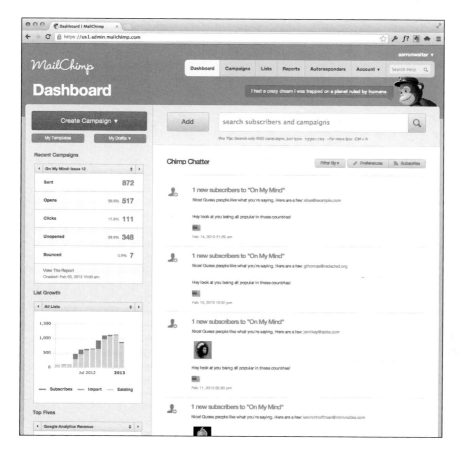

Figure 5.2
MailChimp's design language gives the site its unique personality.

Ask *lots* of questions. To some the word *professional* is associated with sans-serif fonts, the color blue, and a stock image of a smiling woman on a phone, but to others a site like MailChimp is very professional. Some clients have branding guidelines that define the sandbox in which you're required to work. It's the designer's job to translate the client's story into design components that are easily associated with that story. It's hard to do, but hey, that's why they call it *work*. Still, it can be a lot of fun. Play around and test the associations people come up with when they see your design.

This book is about web design workflow, not design, so I won't go on too long about this. But remember that finding a process that lets you develop a design language is very important. You'll pull out the pieces of the language you need to create the story of your website or application.

Serve your design to actual devices

Either you've heard this a lot, or you're going to: *use actual devices to view your design*. Do it no matter where you are in the design process. Put your designs on a web server somewhere and bother people wherever you are by asking them if you could—just for a minute—borrow their unusual device to check out a design. (Only do that with people you know—although it could be a nice way to meet new people, too.)

Later in this book, we'll discuss when and how you can show your design to your clients in an actual browser, on an actual device. Even though you're "just designing," get in the browser.

To do that, you'll need to put your project folder on a web server or serve it locally from your own computer. This allows you to point your (mobile) device's browser to your file. A web server (on the internet) is best, obviously, especially for checking remotely with borrowed devices. If you don't have access to a web server or don't know how to set one up, you can start up a simple ad hoc web server in your project folder as described below.

STARTING AN AD HOC WEB SERVER

If you don't know how to set up a web server or you don't have access to one, you can follow the steps below to start a simple web server that serves your project folder. You'll need to install the Python programming language if it's not installed already. I can really recommend the ad hoc server, which is simple to start up and you can immediately view your design on actual devices, provided they're all running on the same local network.

You'll need to know your computer's IP address on your local network in order to access it from browsers on other devices. One method to find it is to type the following in your terminal:

```
ifconfig | awk '/inet\ / { print $2 }'
```

This command should output a number of IP addresses. In most cases, you'll want to note the one starting with 192.168.

Once you know what your local IP address, you can start a simple web server by executing the following command in your terminal application (from within your project folder—check with `pwd`):

```
$ python -m SimpleHTTPServer 8000
```

This starts a web server that's good enough for our static files at port 8000. You can now open a browser on another device (say, your phone) and enter the following URL:

```
http://[your IP address]:8000
```

Obviously, you'll replace `[your IP address]` with the IP address you noted from the steps above. If all went well, you should see your design on the phone. You can do the same thing with as many devices as you like.

To stop the web server, simply press CTRL-D.

This little command is wonderful, and lets you check your design on any device on your network. Sometimes, an emulator or simulator can be useful.

I know I've said it's critical to test on actual devices, but there may be times when an emulator is useful or times when you have no better option. In general, however, emulators (or simulators) should simply be stand-ins until you're able to test on actual devices, or a way to check things quickly or when device differences are less important (such as when creating the wireframes we made in Chapter 3, "Content Reference Wireframes").

We're starting off with very simple CSS. My expectation is that we'll lose some CSS for older phones, but the structured content will be available and there are some simple changes we can make to our CSS to get the site looking just fine on older phones.

Also, remember that this book is about design process, not development. I won't get into all the things that need to be done to get a site working and looking good on most devices. Our purpose here is to use some development knowledge and techniques in order to:

1. Help designers who've been locked into a visual environment better understand the medium for which they're designing.

2. Enable designers to experience the real-world impact of the design choices they make.

Enhancing your structured content

NOTE
Some mobile browsers both shrink the page *and* put the text into a narrow column.

Now that you've got your device or emulator ready, open the index.html file you generated with Pandoc in Chapter 4, "Designing in Text," in the device's or emulator's browser. This is not what you expected! The page is wide, and the text is very, very small. It appears as if you're looking at a normal desktop web page that's been shrunk down to fit on this browser (**Figure 5.3**). And that's exactly what's happening.

Remember the wireframe we made in Chapter 3? Open that in your mobile browser. Big difference, right? *This* is what the site is supposed to look like.

EMULATORS AND SIMULATORS

Max Firtman provides an excellent definition of the difference between emulators and simulators:

> Generally speaking, an emulator is a piece of software that translates compiled code from an original architecture to the platform where it is running [...] On the other hand, a simulator is a less complex application that simulates some of the behavior of a device, but does not emulate hardware and does not work over the real operating system.

Emulators, in my opinion, are superior to simulators because they more closely reproduce what happens on actual devices. Most mobile emulators and simulators are part of software development kits (SDKs): packages of software for use by app developers for certain platforms. Android has an SDK for Android developers, Apple has an SDK for iOS developers, and so forth. However, web designers and developers can also use them because the phone simulations *contain a web browser.*

SDKs aren't hard to come by, but some involve registration processes and some are just a pain to install. However, they are a great first stop at these very early stages and need to check your progress quickly. There are simulators and emulators of many platforms available. Firtman has one of the best lists I've seen at http://www.mobilexweb.com/emulators.

Figure 5.3
Our Pandoc-generated page doesn't yet look the way it should in a mobile browser.

This all has to do with the differences between the visual viewport and the layout viewport, which we discussed in Chapter 3. If you recall, we used the `meta` element to tell the browser to set the viewport width to the device width. The `index.html` file we got from Pandoc contains only the actual Markdown content converted to HTML; there is no HTML `DOCTYPE` or `<head>` in the document, thus no metadata.

There are two obvious things we could do at this point:

1. Change this HTML file so it contains a `DOCTYPE` and a `<head>` with the `meta` element.

2. Paste the converted content from the Pandoc `index.html` into the wireframe.

The problem with both of these options is that they go against the philosophy of the responsive workflow that making changes should be as easy as possible until as late as possible in the design process. What happens if there are changes to the wireframe? We would be changing both wireframe and content. What happens if we change content? We would be forced to cut and paste small content changes into the appropriate places in the wireframe.

I'd like to keep the HTML as a simple block of markup rather than a complete page, but at this stage I want to test it as a page without combining it with the wireframe (we'll do that in a later chapter). The answer is to use a template.

Introducing templates

Templates are boilerplate pieces of code—containers of code, if you will—into which your code will be "poured." Think of a template as a cup. You create the type of cup you need and pour your markup into it. Our cup, at the moment, is very simple and matches the code we used when we first started creating our wireframe:

```
<!DOCTYPE html>
<html lang="en">
    <head>
        <meta charset="utf-8">
        <meta name="viewport"
        →content="width=device-width,initial-scale=1.0">
        <title>Responsive Design Workflow</title>
        <link rel="stylesheet" href="styles/base.css"
        →media="screen">

    </head>
    <body>
        $body$
    </body>
</html>
```

Type this code into a text editor and save the file with a name that indicates that it's a template (so you remember). I usually create a new folder in my current project folder. I call that folder `templates`, and in it I save this template file as `default.html`.

If you're not familiar with templating, you've probably wondered why the word *body* is in there with the dollar signs on either side. That is called a *variable*, a placeholder for specific content. It's the hollow part of the cup. What do you think will be put into the $body$ variable in this case? Yup, the entire HTML contents of your converted Markdown.

The reason we're using a template is this: the things in the template will *not* often change, but the HTML that's going into $body$ might. More importantly, this template can be used for practically *any* page we design for this project, not just the home page we've been using as an example.

USING THE TEMPLATE WITH PANDOC

To tell Pandoc to use the template, we need to add a little bit to the `pandoc` command we'll be typing:

```
$ pandoc index.markdown --template templates/default.html
→-o index.html
```

Try this out. Make sure you're in the main project folder that contains `index.markdown`. Remember that you can enter the `pwd` command if you're not completely sure which folder you're in, and `cd ..` will take you to the parent folder of the one you're currently in.

NEW TO THE COMMAND LINE?

If these exercises are your first adventure into using the command line, look at the command carefully and try to read it, translated into plain English.

```
pandoc index.markdown --template templates/default.html
→-o index.html
```

It says, "Run Pandoc on `index.markdown`, combine that with the template `default.html` which is in the `templates` folder, and create an output file called `index.html`."

Reading commands in this way helps you not only understand exactly what they do, but also remember them.

Once you've typed the command and hit the Return key, your `index.html` will be replaced with a new one. To confirm this, open the file in a text editor. You should now see your template code, with the converted HTML from your Markdown file between the `<body></body>` tags. If this is not the case, go back through the steps in this chapter and make sure you followed each one exactly.

If you open the new HTML file in your emulator (or access it from your device), you'll see that the page shows up as it should, with the width of the page equal to the width of the device (**Figure 5.4**). This is our starting point.

NOTE
If you're using something other than Pandoc, you'll need to read your converter's documentation to see if templates are supported. If you're a more experienced web developer, you can get creative and use any templating system you like. Pandoc is written in Haskell, but there are template syntaxes for practically every language imaginable. Personally, I like Pandoc's simple dollar sign syntax just fine.

Figure 5.4
The Pandoc-generated page with a proper template applied.

TEMPLATES ARE NOT REQUIRED, BUT THEY'RE USEFUL

Most often, you'll be designing more than one page. While you could always make an HTML file for each different page, you'll be repeating a lot of the information in those files (the stuff we put into the template). Using templates allows you to have a series of Markdown files that contain *only content*, which keeps things nicely separated until you run Pandoc on them. If content changes in one of the files, you simply run Pandoc on that file again. If you decide to change something in the template—the link to the style sheet, for example—you only have to change it in one place and run Pandoc on each of your files again. And there's another benefit: since Markdown is such an easy-to-understand form of markup, you can have content authors prepare them for you.

I realize that for some readers the introduction of templates adds another layer of complexity. I ask you to give it some time to sink in. If you find the "geeky" stuff in this chapter hard to swallow, just let it rest for now and come back and reread the chapter at your leisure. Also, be advised that later chapters will be even geekier, so this is my way of getting your toes in the water, so to speak. All of this more technical stuff is really useful to know—or at least to know about. Should you decide to use some of these tools, they have the potential to increase your effectiveness. And really, nothing we've handled so far is hard to do; it might just be different than what you're used to.

Your project folder so far

Before we start our design work, let's sync up for a minute and make sure your files and folders are set up the way mine are. If you had any problems with the previous sections, these might have been due to trying commands or saving files in the wrong folder. Your project folder should look something like this:

```
project-folder
|- inventory.txt
|- wireframe.html
|- styles
|   |- base.css
|   |- medium.css
|   `- large.css
|- index.markdown
|- index.html
`- templates
    `- default.html
```

NOTE

The names of these files and folders can be tailored to your personal preferences; you'll need to replace the names I've used in various examples with your own.

Think and sketch

Take a good, long look at the content in a mobile browser. Scroll down and think about it. Hopefully, you've already defined goals and values, and are aware of any visual requirements such as branding and identity guidelines (or the personal color preferences of your client—it happens). Don't skip this step.

It's a sign of my age, but I sketch on paper, or on the screen with a Wacom pen tablet (but not in Photoshop). I also sketch on actual devices like phones and tablets with one of those pens designed for touch devices, a neat little trick I learned from Stephanie Rieger (**Figure 5.5**). Used with a full-screen drawing program on the device, these pens are great for sketching actual-size wireframes and thinking about various design options.

That's what I do, but everyone's different.

Now that you have some structured content to look at, you know what it will look like if no CSS is applied. That's your starting point. Now it's time to jump into your own creative process, whether on paper or in a software tool, and start sketching what you want things to look like.

Figure 5.5
Sketching on actual devices is fun and useful.

Full disclosure: This workflow encourages creating mockups for small-screen devices *first*, but that doesn't mean you can't think about and sketch your ideas for larger screens right away. I do that myself, and I find it useful to at least sketch and consider what I'll want things to look like on the desktop. Feel free to do the same.

As I've mentioned, this book is not about how to design; it's about how to visualize your design in the most effective way. Right now, you need to do the most challenging part of this process: design. Think. Sketch. And when you're confident you have some ideas you'd like to mock up, you're ready to continue.

Playing with type and color

One of the biggest problems I have with designing in tools like image editors is the disconnect between the tool and the actual web. Tools like Photoshop create *images*. The web displays *content*, and the rendering varies from platform to platform and browser to browser. It's important to get in the browser as early as possible, so you can see what your design actually does on the web. This will allow you to make adjustments as necessary, potentially giving you the opportunity to improve your designs and, by extension, your skill as a designer.

One of the easiest ways to get started is with type. Typography, as you probably know, is a huge subject, full of complexities. It has been argued that typography is the most important aspect of web design.[5] (It's also one of the most frustrating, as type rendering can vary so drastically on the web.) I find that type is a great place to start designing. Many years ago when I art directed print, the first thing I did on each project was think about type. Let's start with type here as well.

PHOTOSHOP:
NOT COMPLETELY FORBIDDEN

Several years ago I did a series of guest lectures at a college in the Netherlands. The first thing that struck me is that the students literally couldn't wait to jump into Photoshop. Heresy! How dare they!

But when I took a closer look, I saw that this was simply their style of sketching. They open Photoshop and experiment. They think on the screen. It wasn't for me, but it worked for them. If you happen to "think" in Photoshop, or any other computer application, this workflow doesn't require you to stop doing that.

I simply want you to use more appropriate tools for creating the design comps you will show to both developers and your clients. While I have my reservations about thinking in software—for example, the tendency of some people to let their design choices be led by the capabilities of the software—I respect everyone's individual creative process.

---

5 Oliver Reichenstein, "Web Design is 95% Typography." *iA Blog*. http://informationarchitects.net/blog/the-web-is-all-about-typography-period.

The first thing I'd ask you to think about is whether the majority of your type will be in a serif or a sans-serif font. If you've already sketched out a design, you'll most likely have made that choice by now. For our book site example, I've chosen to go with a sans-serif typeface, since I've seen the comps for the book's cover, which also use sans-serif type. This informed my decision, the same way typographical guidelines from a style manual might lead your decision in a given project.

We're going to specify a *font stack* for the page we're working on, based on the choice for a sans-serif typeface.

We specify the font stack in base.css. Open that file and take a look at it; you'll see the wireframes styles we had put in there. Those style declarations were *namespaced*; they apply only to HTML elements with the class wireframe. We want our type to apply universally, so we don't need to namespace. *Above* the wireframe styles, type in the following declaration:

```
body {
    font-size: 100%;
    font-family: Gill Sans, Helvetica, Arial, sans-serif;
}
h1,h2,h3,h4,h5,h6 {
    font-weight: 200;
}
```

Please note that these styles are for our example site; for your own design you would use the font declarations of your choice.

When you refresh the page in your browser, you'll see the font styles applied. If you're looking at the page in a desktop browser, make the browser window narrow, so it approximates the width of a smartphone. I would recommend opting for an emulator as we discussed earlier.

START SCULPTING

For your own project, you should have made some sketches by now and know how you want your design to look. For most web designers, this is the point in the workflow when you'd normally start working in Photoshop, with two differences:

1. Instead of working in Photoshop you'll continue working with CSS, possibly changing something in your HTML every once in a while.

2. You'll be applying styles incrementally, such that their cumulative effect will be to visualize the design(s) you've sketched. You'll do this by starting with the narrow screen design using simple CSS.

The first part of creating your responsive design is the linear design, the application of simple CSS (namely, type and color) to create the base styles that will be used with all screen widths. This means no layout yet, as that applies only to screens large enough and browsers capable of showing it. The key in this phase is to go just one small step further than Bryan Rieger's method. We're still communicating with HTML, but it's no longer unstyled HTML.

The idea is to start **sculpting** the unstyled HTML until you get the typography and color treatment on par with your design sketches. Do it methodically. Add to your CSS only if it contributes to the design, with perhaps some simple margins and padding. You can add background colors if you like, but here are some things I prefer to avoid at this stage:

- Any form of layout whatsoever (no columns!)
- CSS effects such as box-shadows, text-shadows, border-radius, and gradients
- Font embedding (`@font-face`)

So, to be clear, *in this phase we're simply setting the stage for more complex CSS later*. We want something that reads like a linear document but which has some type and color applied to it. You'll be implementing your full-blown design in later steps. Easy does it.

Sculpting is simply the word I use to describe the act of turning a page of stacked content into a linear design. It's a matter of many small, incremental changes—margins here, padding there, type choices—which together transform visually boring content into something with a distinct style.

ADD SOME IMAGES

You probably want some images in your design. This includes things like a company logo, photographs, or icons. This is a good time to put these into your mockup. For images that are actually part of the content (read: not background images), the right place for those is in the HTML. Put them *where they make the most sense if this linear layout were the only layout available.* Obviously, you can create or edit these images in Photoshop or another image editor. After all, that's what image editors were made for.

Try to create versions of your images that fit into this linear design on a small device. In other words, don't make large images and shrink them with HTML or CSS. Actually create versions of the images that are the correct size for your current reference device. It's advisable to start with a larger image and export it as a smaller image from your image editor of choice. This lets you experiment and see how large or small your images need to be on a small screen. That is valuable information.

NOTE

It could be that the developer(s) will later choose to use only one image, but performance is extremely important on all devices, and in the event you eventually do need multiple sizes of an image, you'll be ready.

HEY, WAIT, YOU'RE ASKING ME TO DO CSS

That is correct. Fashion designers work with actual fabrics. Furniture designers prototype their design with actual materials. Why? Because they can, and they want to know what *experience* their designs will bring to the people who use them. Web design is something you experience, not something you see a picture of in a book or behind glass.

If you design for the web, knowing only a few CSS tricks and design patterns you've seen others use won't cut it. You can't simply make pretty pictures of how you want a website to look. You need to experience it first—in different environments, on different devices, in different browsers—so you know what you're actually creating for others.

Photoshop is a design tool. So is CSS. So is a web browser. So is your phone. It's that simple. If you've ever wondered about the "should web designers also be able to code" debate, wonder no more. The answer is yes—within reason, of course.

FORM ELEMENTS AND TOUCH DEVICES

Assuming your small-screen reference device is a touch device, and if you have forms in your design (or you're designing a web application and have various UI elements such as buttons), this is the time to start getting a feel for how big these things really are. You can almost always make them larger. This goes for type as well. Don't do anything with layout just yet, but you can play with the dimensions of things. Adjust until it feels right, until it feels comfortable when touching the element with your finger (if you try it on at least one device, which I can't stress enough). Think about the amount of white space between elements (above and below). Adjust until you have a clean, usable linear design on your reference device.

Don't do too much just yet

When you've looked at your linear design on a mobile device, look at it again on another, different device. What's different? Note some of the issues you might have with certain types of devices; change small things as necessary. And remember, don't do too much at this point—no layout allowed.

When you're satisfied with the result, you should have an HTML document that reads in a linear fashion and contains some basic styling of structural elements using some of the color and type ideas you sketched (**Figure 5.6**).

Figure 5.6
The book site linear design on a mobile device.

In the next chapter, we'll look at how to set the stage for making the design responsive, by estimating and visualizing various *breakpoints:* the points the design will *respond to* when various conditions are met.

I've mentioned that the way the content behaves within a certain context should determine the breakpoints. In preparation for thinking about these breakpoints (and breakpoints in general), I recommend using your linear design to start exploring at what points you think your design might need to change.

View your linear design on as many devices as you can and see how the content looks at various screen sizes. Are the text columns too narrow? Too wide? Does the text remain readable, or is it too small on some devices?

You might even want to jot down some notes about your breakpoint studies for use in the next step. Breakpoints need not denote big layout changes, even small things might need to change. Indeed, one breakpoint might only trigger some text resizing. Try to get a feel for what needs to be done, and use your browser's developer tools to play around with possible changes.

This exploration is optional, but can help you going forward. And now, breakpoints!

## 6

BREAKPOINT GRAPHS

"The most important function of a spec is to design the program."

—JOEL SPOLSKY

You may have noticed a common thread running through the steps in the responsive design workflow: the deliverables in each step are primarily meant to *aid* the design process as opposed to being client-centric deliverables *based on* a hidden design process. Another characteristic of the workflow deliverables is that most of them can be construed as a form of documentation, whether on their own or in combination with the results of other steps in the workflow. Joel Spolsky, in a blog post that's as relevant today as it was when he wrote it in 2000, said:

> "Writing a spec is a great way to nail down all those irritating design decisions, large and small, that get covered up if you don't have a spec. Even small decisions can get nailed down with a spec."[1]

A **specification** is a form of documentation that describes how something should work, and how it should be implemented. Thus, a CSS spec describes how CSS should be implemented in browsers by the browser makers (the implementers, in this case).

The word *documentation* (or variants like **specification**, or *spec*) doesn't excite many people, although I've known some who *love* creating it. The word conjures up images of hours or days of writing, of describing the way things work in horrific detail. The oft-heard saying "a picture is worth a thousand words," however, suggests that documentation needn't always read like an instruction manual. This is especially true of breakpoint graphs, the topic of this chapter.

Looking back on the previous steps in the workflow, you can see that the deliverables not only help create the design, but also can be incorporated into the design documentation. For this documentation to be seamless and make more sense to the reader, you'll need to write some background on the project and tie the various steps together. However, much of the documentation can be surprisingly visual.

The content inventory is documentation in and of itself, and can also serve as part of a much larger documentation suite. This also applies to content reference wireframes and structured text designs. While not every workflow deliverable is useful as standalone documentation, each somehow documents a part of the design process. We'll look at how to tie all these deliverables together to create overarching design documentation later in this book.

---

1 *Painless Functional Specifications—Part 1: Why Bother?* http://www.joelonsoftware.com/articles/fog0000000036.html

Whenever possible, I prefer to go the visual route when creating documentation. You may have also found in your own projects that documentation containing images seems much more effective.

Aside from the fact that accessibility concerns may lead you to write everything in detail anyway, many things can be communicated *more* clearly with images. And even if you write everything out, *starting* with images might help clarify what you need to write.

This same principle applies to both user documentation and design documentation. I dare say that most designers are familiar with identity/branding guidelines, commonly called *style manuals* or *style guides* at the time of this writing. These documents traditionally describe which elements are available for an organization's visual identity (logos, type, illustrations, and so on), under what circumstances each can be used, and *how* each of these elements should be used. I've seen style manuals that were hundreds of pages long. What gets you through these manuals, as a reader, is the fact that they're so visual. There's a *textual description* of how white space should be used with the logo, as well as a *picture*, complete with measurements. The important point here is that any accompanying text should provide additional details that cannot be conveyed through an image. (At worst, the text can be completely unnecessary, save for reasons of making this information accessible to those who can't understand the image for whatever reason.) In any case,

NOTE

Terms like identity guidelines and style guides often refer to the same thing, but not always. People often interchange these terms and their meanings, perhaps a result of the convergence of the development and design fields.

TRAINING DOCUMENTATION

My company once took on a project for a group of large government organizations, each of which wanted a web application that would make it possible to publish legislation for its geographical region on the web. The members of the client team were very happy with the result, but they already knew how everything worked, having gone through the entire process. The tens of people who would be entering new legislation had no such advantage, and instead had to learn everything from scratch. So we organized half-day workshops to get the editors up to speed. Everyone seemed to get it—until the next day. Then came the emails and phone calls. We pointed them to the in-app documentation: small chapters of content describing how to do common tasks. This helped, but not significantly. So we added more and better screenshots of all the steps in the process and made a couple of screencasts. That did the trick.

we should start with an image where possible, and then describe what that image means in text. This can be a *huge* time-saver and make for much more effective documentation.

Documentation for breakpoints

I have a thing for data visualization. I don't mean those modified bar charts you see in newspapers where the bars are replaced with barrels of oil or whatever else is being measured. I mean visually simple and clear expressions of data presented in a way that helps the reader understand that data intuitively, often without explanation—the kind of visualization that lets the reader gain insight or draw conclusions from the data based on that understanding.

And since it's all about understanding, the visualizations should not be fancy (to impress) or unnecessarily complex.

A **breakpoint graph** is a graphic depiction of various breakpoints and the changes that occur at these breakpoints within a responsive design.

Breakpoint graphs are my way of visualizing breakpoints. They start as design tools and become a form of documentation. As in the earlier steps in the workflow, I start with educated guesses in the initial design phase and make reality-based revisions later.

But before we get into breakpoint graphs and how to create them, it's important to be clear on the definition of a breakpoint.

Anatomy of a breakpoint

Breakpoints are often described as the points at which CSS media queries are activated and thus when changes to the page styles are applied. While this is a true statement, it's not a full definition. A broader, technology-independent definition can be helpful.

I've come to define breakpoints as *the points when certain aspects of a website or web application change depending on specified conditions*. Three factors are candidates for change when a breakpoint is reached:

1. Aspects of visual design and layout
2. Aspects of functionality
3. Aspects of content

These things might need to change (or you might *want* them to change) based on various conditions. The points at which those conditions are *true* are breakpoints. Here's an example in plain language:

"When the viewport width is at least 600 pixels wide, use a two-column layout instead of a one-column layout."

This follows the simple syntax of "if [condition], then [change]." Again, the point at which the condition is true is the breakpoint, in this case, when the viewport is at least 600px wide. This makes understanding the CSS media query syntax easy:

```
@media only screen and (min-width: 600px) {
    /* Do stuff */
}
```

This should be pretty easy to read. The only keyword simply "hides" the media query from browsers that don't support it. Other than that, the query simply reads:

"When using a screen with a viewport that is at least 600px wide, do stuff."

Another reason to consider a more full definition of breakpoints is that CSS is not the only method used to implement changes when a breakpoint has been reached. JavaScript can also be used to determine this. The following examples mean basically the same thing as the CSS media query above:

```
if (document.documentElement.clientWidth >= 600) {
    // Do stuff
}
```

or

```
if (window.matchMedia("(min-width: 600px)").matches) {
    // Do stuff
}
```

NOTE

Be aware that the "media queries" in JavaScript are evaluated only once by the browser, while CSS media queries are evaluated continually.

In general, it shouldn't matter how you do it. The important thing is that you'll most likely have several different ways of testing conditions, and several things you'll want to change based on those conditions. On complex sites, these conditions and changes are worth keeping track of. Even on simple websites, documenting breakpoints is a useful practice.

While on-breakpoint changes in web projects fall into the aforementioned categories (visual design/layout, functionality, and content), there are few limits on what can constitute a breakpoint. Media features available in CSS media queries—width and device orientation, for example—are just the beginning (though not all enjoy enough browser support). Support for technologies like JavaScript might also be included in your strategy. Device features such as a camera might determine which functions are available to an application. There are many possibilities for breakpoints, not all of which can be triggered by CSS.

This implies that there are a *lot* of different things to consider when determining breakpoints. Some of them are marginally related to design. All of them have *something* to do with design; the designer should at least know what effects breakpoint changes will have on the whole experience. Determining breakpoints is, once again, a team effort.

PROGRESSIVE ENHANCEMENT USES IMPLICIT BREAKPOINTS

We've actually been using breakpoints for years: "when JavaScript is available, do JavaScript stuff." If you practice progressive enhancement, this concept will already be familiar to you. You might not have thought about these conditions as breakpoints, but it can be helpful to do so. A good chunk of client-side functionality is available only on user agents that have JavaScript support. So in the same way that you'd say, "Give me a new layout when the window gets wide enough," you can also say, "Enhance my simple HTML form with AJAX-support and other functionality when JavaScript is available." Documenting these things can be useful for many reasons, not the least of which is having a map that can show you potential holes in your support for browsers and devices.

Figure 6.1
Bullet graphs were created to communicate a large amount of information in a small amount of space.

Visualizing breakpoints

I've often found myself writing breakpoints in a simple table format. As a big fan of data visualization, I was excited to come across Stephen Few's bullet graph specification (**Figure 6.1**).[2]

A bullet graph is a type of bar graph that (to me, at least) resembles a thermometer. They can be placed either horizontally or vertically. They combine a quantitative scale with qualitative ranges and use markers for specific measures.

Bullet graphs were developed for data dashboards, such as those used by sales teams, so they have virtually nothing in common with responsive design breakpoints. However, I liked how bullet graphs included so much information in such a small amount of space. Could I make something similar to describe breakpoints in a visual manner? Sure, a spreadsheet might work, but hey, I'm a visual guy. Hence, the breakpoint graph.

Breakpoint graphs are an easy way to visualize progressive enhancement: from basic HTML to the most advanced CSS and JavaScript, from simple to complex, from a list of addresses to an interactive map, and, of course, from small screen layouts to large screen layouts.

Breakpoint graph components

My breakpoint graphs usually contain only a small number of simple components (**Table 6.1**).

With quantitative scale, I'm referring to a simple ordinal scale such as *small*, *medium*, and *large*. The horizontal line represents this scale, which is arbitrary and can be whatever you need it to be depending on what you're communicating with your breakpoint graph (**Figure 6.2**). In its obvious form, the horizontal line would imply a scale of viewport widths from, say, 0px to >1280px or 0em to >50em or something similar.

0   > 1280

Figure 6.2
A horizontal line represents a quantitative scale.

2 http://en.wikipedia.org/wiki/Bullet_graph

Table 6.1 Typical breakpoint graph components

COMPONENT	USED FOR
Horizontal line	Quantitative scale
Bands or blocks	Qualitative ranges
Points/markers	Breakpoints
Text	Labels for breakpoints Labels for scale Labels for ranges Annotations
Images	Layout thumbnails, for example

Qualitative ranges have no intrinsic order; indeed, they may have nothing to do with one another. You may have bands or blocks that represent "when JavaScript is available" or "the device has a camera" (**Figure 6.3**). Not all ranges will map directly to your chosen quantitative scale. For example, viewport width has nothing directly to do with the amount of JavaScript support. Thus, your horizontal line and colored blocks or bands should somehow be related. Otherwise, you might need more than one breakpoint graph, which we'll discuss shortly.

The actual breakpoints (the points at which changes in your design will take place) are placed as markers on the horizontal line—and thus also on top of your blocks or bands—to indicate where the change takes place (**Figure 6.4**). The bands and lines are conditions; the markers indicate the change points. The number of breakpoints will vary by project, and whether or not you choose to include major breakpoints (huge changes) and minor breakpoints (changes to specific elements) in the same graph.

Figure 6.3
Blocks or bands represent qualitative ranges.

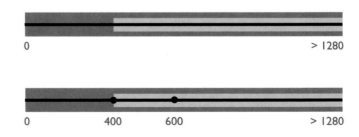

0   > 1280

Figure 6.4
Breakpoint markers with labels can be added for clarity.

0   400   600   > 1280

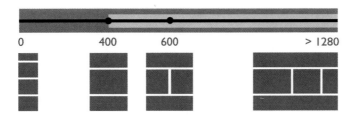

Figure 6.5
Thumbnail images
visualize layout
changes.

Of course, you'll usually want to label your breakpoints and may include an annotation or two for clarity.

Small pictures can be used to visually indicate the types of changes that will take place. This increases the physical size of the graph, but makes up for it in communicative impact. Thumbnail images of layout changes, for example, make it immediately clear what will happen at a given breakpoint and can eliminate the need for detailed textual explanation (**Figure 6.5**).

In practice you'll use only the components you need, and you might add some of your own. However you do it, try to keep your breakpoint graphs as simple as possible.

After extolling the virtues of images as an effective way to communicate, it's probably about time for a visual example. Let's take a look at how we would make a simple breakpoint graph for the book site.

Creating a simple breakpoint graph

As with all steps in this book, I encourage you to follow along with the examples. Even if you decide not to use a specific idea, following along is very useful; it helps you understand exactly what's going on and lets you experience the potential advantages or drawbacks of a particular approach for your own projects and style of working. As always, the Tool Rule applies here: use the tool you feel most comfortable with. Since breakpoint graphs are visuals, an image editor or illustration application would work perfectly. Who knows, you might even prefer to sketch them first with pen and paper! What a thought!

When you create breakpoint graphs for the first time in the design process, it will mainly be guesswork based on experience. Once you've started working on your web-based comp, you can base your estimates on the way the content is rendered. When dealing with breakpoints based on viewport widths (obviously common in responsive design), the temptation is to start off with actual device screen sizes. I strongly discourage this practice. In his article *Fanfare for the Common Breakpoint*, Jeremy Keith wrote,

---

"If we begin with some specific canvases (devices), they're always going to be arbitrary. There are so many different screen sizes and ratios out there that it doesn't make sense to favour a handful of them out of tradition. 320, 480, 640… those numbers aren't any more special than any other screen widths."[3]

The fact is that we don't know which devices people will use to interact with our websites now or in the future, even if we convince ourselves otherwise. This is true not only for viewport widths, but also for other factors such as various device capabilities. Keith sums it up nicely later in the same article:

"I think our collective obsession with trying to nail down 'common' breakpoints has led to a fundamental misunderstanding about the nature of responsive design: it's not about what happens at the breakpoints—it's about what happens between the breakpoints."

---

3 http://adactio.com/journal/5425/

This is why I tend to "default guess" breakpoints at 600px and 900px in the beginning. These values have little to do with specific devices. I've even used them in media queries of actual projects because they happened to work so well. It really will depend on your project. Almost always, I end up converting the values to ems (see Tip).[4]

Moving on to our example, let's create a breakpoint graph that describes major layout changes based on viewport width.

First, draw a horizontal line. Try not to quiver at this extremely difficult step. This horizontal line will be your scale. In this case, it will show the units you're using for the viewport width. If you're using pixels, the leftmost point of the line represents 0px. In responsive design, the rightmost point often represents the last breakpoint before "infinite," as in "greater than 1000px" or something similar, but if your design suddenly "stops" for whatever reason, you can just end your responsive universe at your measure of choice.

Now place some points where you think the breakpoints will be. Don't worry about being wrong; you'll most certainly change these breakpoints later *because your content will tell you to*. Place the points more or less on the correct place on your scale. For example, if your scale is from 0px to (>)1000px and you have a breakpoint at 500px, place your point in the middle of the horizontal line. Label the points (**Figure 6.6**).

That was easy, right?

Now that you've shown where the breakpoints are, you need to indicate what will happen at those breakpoints. This is, after all, part of your design documentation! For this particular type of graph, I like to use thumbnail images based on the content reference wireframes (**Figure 6.7**). These are simple, easy to make, and easy to understand.

TIP

When designing responsively, consider using ems as opposed to pixels for your scale (and thus for your media queries later on). There's nothing wrong with pixels (especially in this phase), but ems have their advantages when used correctly.

0px   500px   1000px

Figure 6.6
A breakpoint graph with breakpoints added and labeled.

---

4 Read Lyza Gardner's wonderful little post on em-based media queries at http://blog.cloudfour.com/the-ems-have-it-proportional-media-queries-ftw/.

Figure 6.7
The breakpoint graph with layout thumbnails added.

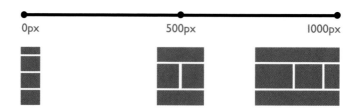

Chartjunk refers to visual elements in charts and graphs that are not necessary for the reader to comprehend the information represented in the graph, or that distract the reader from this information.

This graph already communicates a reasonable amount of information in a relatively small space, and is understandable with no textual explanation or **chartjunk**.[5] For smaller or less complex websites, this might be all you need. Many projects, though, will require more information.

Major and minor breakpoints

So far we've marked only *major* breakpoints: those points where changes have an impact on, as in the previous example, the whole layout. But there are many potential minor breakpoints. It could be that certain elements on the page change in some way at a certain point, while the rest of the page remains the same. This is often the case when a page is still wide enough to keep a given page layout, where one block of content still must switch from a single column of text to multiple columns and vice versa. Or consider that when a column becomes slightly too small to render navigation horizontally, some change to that navigation is made (smaller type, moved under the logo, whatever) while the general design of the page remains the same.

While this book is about responsive design workflow, it's not about the basics of responsive design, in which fluid layout plays an important role. Much of the flexibility "between the breakpoints" to which Jeremy Keith refers is afforded us by fluid layout. Switching between several fixed-width layouts is not *responsive design*.[6]

These breakpoints can also be included in your breakpoint graph, though I recommend creating a visual differentiation between major and minor breakpoint markers (**Figure 6.8**).

---

5 http://en.wikipedia.org/wiki/Chartjunk

6 To learn more about fluid layout and the basics of responsive design, read Ethan Marcotte's article on the subject at http://www.alistapart.com/articles/responsive-web-design/. His book *Responsive Web Design* (A Book Apart, 2011) is also invaluable.

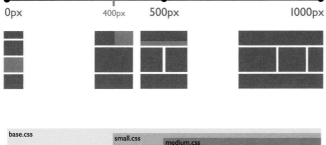

Figure 6.8
The breakpoint graph with minor breakpoints added.

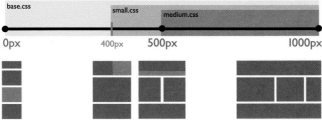

Figure 6.9
The breakpoint graph now shows which CSS files are applied at which breakpoints.

It's also possible to use color-filled areas to indicate major content or functionality changes, or to emphasize them. These areas are useful for indicating *ranges* within which certain conditions apply. This can be anything. For example, we might want to indicate which CSS files are applied at any given screen width (**Figure 6.9**). Ranges are a great way to do this, although this is a simple example. Ranges become even more useful when mapping things other than width-related factors.

Adding more complexity

For complex projects, a single breakpoint graph might not be enough. You could try it, but it would become very cluttered, which defeats the whole purpose of the breakpoint graph in the first place. For these complex situations—and because breakpoint graphs take up relatively little space—I recommend making more than one for different aspects of the design and stacking them on top of one another.

Remember the basic things a breakpoint graph communicates:

1. What is going to change

2. What conditions trigger those changes

Let's say you want to graph functionality based on device capabilities in addition to layout changes. You could plot layout to screen widths on one graph, and content to capabilities on another. This is a good idea, since the one doesn't necessarily have anything to do with the other. Let's examine that with a more complex example.

A more complex example: A podcast player

Let's say our client publishes podcasts, and would like a podcast player on her website. The display of an audio player is not possible in every situation, but the conditions have little or nothing to do with the width of the viewport. In this case, we choose to graph the changes in layout in one graph and the progressive enhancement scheme for the audio player in another graph.

The layout graph is done exactly as in our previous example, so there's no need to repeat that exercise. We'll focus on the graph for the audio player. At first glance, this might seem technical to some designers, something best left to developers to handle: just design a nice-looking audio player and be done with it. Sure, you could do that. But if you share my opinion that the design of contingencies is *also* part of design, read on.

In this case, we'll use the breakpoint graph as a tool to think about and plan our progressive enhancement strategy for this audio player. When we're done, we'll have documentation of that strategy.

As always, it's important to consider the restraints. In this case, the client has only MP3 files and doesn't want to convert them or use any alternate formats. Also, the whole project team and client have opted for HTML5 audio when possible, with a Flash or Silverlight player fallback when possible.

Let's think about what this means:

1. Some devices/browsers have no support for HTML5 audio, and no support for Flash or Silverlight. For these, you might like to present the user with a download link, perhaps in the form of a button. Upon the user's touching or clicking the button, many devices will ask the user how and with which application they'd like to open the file, offering the device's default player as an option. Some devices, depending on the settings, will open an MP3

file automatically in the device's default player. This will be your base functionality: a link works everywhere HTML is supported. This default will *also* be used in cases where HTML5 audio *is* supported but the browser does not support the MP3 format.

2. Some browsers will support Flash or Silverlight but not HTML5 audio (or HTML5 audio but not MP3). We'll provide these browsers with Flash or Silverlight players (which look like the HTML5 audio player), respectively. We'll basically "fake" HTML5 support with these technologies. We'll use JavaScript to determine which support is available and apply the corresponding technology.

3. Some browsers support HTML5 audio *and* the MP3 format. These will get our shiny HTML5 player.

Now, you could simply write all this down, but I just wrote it, and it's tough even for me to get my head around the plan, let alone a client. You could make a flowchart, but that's not as cool. You've already used a breakpoint graph to describe layout changes, so creating one for the audio player gives you a way to consistently visualize any type of progressive enhancement.

To graph this, start off once again with a horizontal line. This time the horizontal line represents the range of "least capable" browser to "most capable" browser, with the least capable applying the accessible default (the link/button) and the most capable applying the HTML5 audio player. Before you insert the breakpoint markers, though, add some qualitative ranges using rectangular areas to indicate device capabilities or feature support.

What are these ranges? For one, JavaScript is necessary for pretty much every option you can think of except the plain old Download button (**Figure 6.10**). In the same way, MP3 support is needed for all but the button.

SUPPORT javascript

download link

Figure 6.10
The base functionality consists of a Download button, which is replaced when JavaScript is available.

Figure 6.11
The breakpoint graph with capability ranges added.

Figure 6.12
Completed break-point graph of the audio player.

Next, there's a range where Flash and/or Silverlight is supported. And finally, there's a range of browsers supporting HTML5 audio (and MP3) (**Figure 6.11**).

With the ranges in place, it's fairly easy to place the breakpoints; they're typically on the starting end of the range of conditions that trigger them. To add extra visual clarity, you could add some small images indicating how the audio will be handled at the various breakpoints (**Figure 6.12**).

There you have it, a visualization of a progressive enhancement strategy for dealing with an HTML5 audio player. While it's not about screen widths, it's still about being responsive, and there are still breakpoints—even though the breakpoints here have nothing to do with layout. This is so much clearer than a textual description of how you'll deal with the audio player under specific conditions. As a bonus, these visuals encourage you to consider an *accessible* approach to design, and can alert you to contingencies you otherwise might not have considered.

What we've covered

In this chapter, we discussed what breakpoint graphs are and how to draw them, including:

◆ The importance of documentation

◆ The importance of *visuals* in documentation

◆ What a *breakpoint* is

◆ What a breakpoint graph is, and what components comprise a breakpoint graph

◆ The difference between major and minor breakpoints

◆ How to create a simple breakpoint graph to visualize layout changes at various viewport widths

◆ How to use breakpoint graphs to visualize progressive enhancement strategies for non-layout-related factors like device capabilities

Now that you've guesstimated your breakpoints (probably based on the design sketches you've made and your original wireframes), everything's set for revisiting your major layout breakpoints and revising or finishing up your design thoughts for those specific points. In the next chapter, we'll cover a brief step in this workflow in which you'll combine your linear design and your original wireframes to analyze the feasibility of your estimated breakpoints, and simultaneously prepare to create web-based comps.

So, get ready to jump back into some HTML and CSS!

## 7

DESIGNING FOR BREAKPOINTS

"Don't wait for the muse to inspire you, to put you in the mood. That comes only with doing. So do."

—DANNY GREGORY, *THE CREATIVE LICENSE*

So far, this book has been about a workflow that supports your creative process. It's a support system. While it can give you some guidance and the proper space in which to be creative, it does not in and of itself provide that creativity.

This means that when it comes down to it, if you're a visual designer, now's the time to get down to business. This step in the process is where you do the things you're used to doing: sketching, fiddling around in Photoshop, cutting out pieces of paper and rearranging them on the table, drawing on whiteboards (or other available surfaces), and iterating until you have a visual design that pleases you, your boss, and your client.

You'll be experimenting with applying your *design language* at various break-points, thinking all the while about what your design will be doing *between* the breakpoints, as Jeremy Keith notes.[1]

If you've been following along, you'll have done some sketching while working on your linear design. Perhaps you've roughed out what you might want to do at larger screen sizes. Great! If you worked only on your linear or small-screen design and waited until now to sketch for different breakpoints, that's fine too. Personally, I take the latter approach, as it eases me into the visual design process.

Let's get started!

First, a bit about sketching

Sketching, in my opinion, is the single most important skill in a visual designer's repertoire. It's the trick up the magician's sleeve. It's often said that the generation of good ideas is a numbers game: the more sketches you make, the greater the chance that you'll find a high-quality solution. This is true in my own experience: every project I've done well was born out of a serious amount of sketching. Projects that were, shall we say, *less* well done (read: projects that sucked really, really badly) were the ones for which I sketched *less*.

In your *first* sketches, this has very little to do with time; you can do a hundred thumbnails in less than 15 minutes. They won't all be great, but that's not the point of sketching.

1   Jeremy Keith, "Fanfare for the common breakpoint." http://adactio.com/journal/5425/

The point is this: sketching is thinking on a surface. It's liberating and wonderful, especially if you remind yourself that *no one has to see your sketches at all, ever*. You can always choose the ones you show later on. The more I sketch, the more creative I feel. And I never do it enough. Think about the most creative people you know. Chances are, they sketch.

How to sketch

When it comes to sketching, there are no set rules. Coming from advertising design during the time before Photoshop was widely used, I've known plenty of people who sketched with professional-quality colored markers. I've known designers who sketch everything in storyboard form or comic book style. Some use watercolor paints. Some jump straight into Photoshop. Some use a mouse. Some use a tablet.

It doesn't matter. What matters is that you sketch in a form and with tools that let you express your ideas sufficiently, such that the person who needs to work from those sketches can do so effectively. If that person is you, then as long as you know what you meant by whatever you drew, you're doing just fine.

That said, there are some practices I find helpful in my own work that you might find useful as well. My favorite method of sketching parallels the workflow described in this book: it builds from abstract to concrete. If you're a designer, you'll be familiar with this popular method:

1. Start with many small, non-detailed thumbnail sketches.

2. Select the sketches that represent ideas you'd like to further explore.

3. Make more detailed and larger but still rough sketches of the selected ideas.

4. Create realistic comps of the winning rough sketches.

THUMBNAIL SKETCHES: QUANTITY MATTERS

Thumbnail sketches, so named because they're usually quite small, are meant to start exploring many ideas quickly (**Figure 7.1**). No, they don't need to be the size of an actual human thumbnail. But make them small enough that it's impossible to add too much detail. Thumbnails should be done as quickly as possible. They're the lone sketcher's equivalent of a brainstorming session; it's a numbers game, remember? Quantity matters, as does speed. It's often said that the quality of your resulting design ideas will increase as the number

NOTE
If enough time goes by and my sketches are really rough, it's like I'm looking at an alien language and I have no idea what I meant. Have you ever had that experience? Rough is good, but try to sketch clearly enough that your drawing doesn't lose meaning over time.

Figure 7.1
Thumbnail sketches are the perfect way to explore lots of ideas very quickly.
(Image courtesy of Mike Rohde)

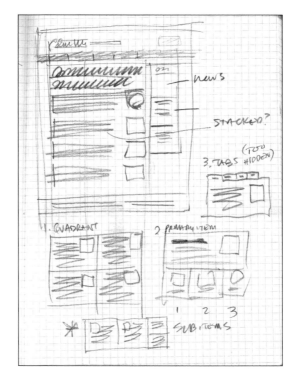

of ideas you generate increases. Assuming this is true, it's most certainly due to the fact that with a large amount of thumbnail sketches, you've considered more options, moved past the clichés (the first ideas that pop into your head are probably similar to the first ideas others have had), and have a larger selection of ideas to choose from. This is all good for your design.

Contrary to conventional wisdom, brainstorming by yourself is more effective than brainstorming with others.[2] You needn't be afraid of coming up with ideas that aren't good enough. *Thumbnail sketches are a design tool, not a deliverable.* They don't have to be pretty. Most of mine look like something you'd find in the trash. In fact, most of them end up there at the end of the day. As you're working, remember that you don't have to show them to anyone else. They're just a means of getting your first ideas on paper, so there's no need to censor yourself. Think like a fashion photographer: make a ton of shots, because most of them will suck. The more you have, the higher the likelihood that you'll find a non-sucky one in there somewhere.

2   Richard Wiseman, *59 Seconds: Think a little, change a lot* (Knopf, 2009).

Remember that anything goes—crazy or unrealistic ideas are OK, since they might lead to more exciting and creative design choices later on. But you'll need to find a balance with speed. I usually challenge myself to get 20 thumbnails done in one minute. That's only three seconds per sketch, so I never make it. But it does get me working at a high tempo. If that seems too much for you, aim for 20 sketches in five minutes. Include just enough information in each sketch so you'll remember your idea when you review the sketches later. Don't stop at 20 sketches, either. Keep going until you feel like there are no ideas left in your brain. Like there's no brain left in your head. Like there's— all right, you get the idea.

What should you sketch? Basically, anything that comes to mind. That said, I do recommend sketching in sets, with each set focusing on the same design components. If you're thinking about layout, do a set of thumbnails that explore layout so that you exhaust your layout ideas. The same goes for the general concept, color, font, or anything worth sketching. You can combine these components in your sketches, but don't just do one set of twenty thumbnails with five layouts, five colors, five fonts, and five images. That's cheating badly. Shame.

Spend no more than, say, 15 minutes on thumbnails, and get as many done as quickly as you can within that amount of time. Like push-ups, the last couple of ideas will hurt the most and be the hardest to do, but they'll have the greatest effect.

Ballpoint pen, fine liner, computer stylus, brush, pencil, paper, napkin, canvas, whiteboard, tablet—it doesn't matter what you use, really, as long as it works for you, not against you, in getting your ideas recorded. Don't focus on tools here; focus on the ideas.

Feel free to annotate your sketches, but keep the notes to a minimum and do them quickly.

MAKE A SELECTION

When you've finished sketching, it's time to make a selection. I like to choose three thumbnails that represent the best ideas from my set of thumbnails. Why three? One or two choices might not allow for enough variety or exploration, and more than three simply take more time to flesh out. Three is a good number to start out with. If none of the three ideas are approved, you can always go back to the thumbnails and pick the three *next best* ideas to further explore.

Once you choose your winning thumbnails, consider each one for a moment. Are there additional annotations you'd like to make? Any notes to yourself about some aspect of the design to serve as reminders once you get into the design in more detail? Jot these down on or near each sketch.

ROUGH SKETCHES: STILL A ROUGH IMPRESSION, BUT QUALITY MATTERS

Next, redraw each of the winning thumbnail ideas in the form of a rough sketch (**Figure 7.2**). For some, any sketch is a rough sketch, even thumbnails. But these roughs are bigger, with more detail. I tend to use a whole sheet of A4 paper for a rough sketch, leaving enough margin space for annotations. Don't be afraid to annotate; write notes to yourself about everything you'd like to explore further, as well as things you don't want to forget.

You don't need to draw text, although you may want to actually read top-level headings and navigation, if they're important to you. Rough sketches usually show more detail and make more use of shading to indicate color differences, backgrounds, and other things that might create contrast. The quality of rough sketches, as far as detail is concerned, is more important than with thumbnails: it's likely that you'll want to use these as discussion pieces within your team so that you can come to an agreement about which design you'll choose for your final mockup.

Figure 7.2
Rough sketches go a step further than thumbnails, with ideas explored more thoroughly. (Image courtesy of Mike Rohde)

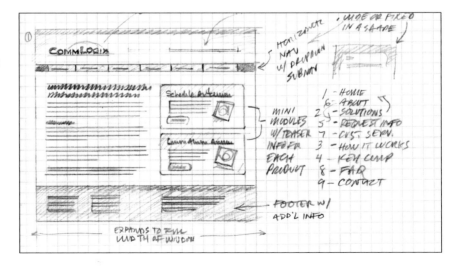

Again, everyone's sketching style is different, and the easier it is for people to interpret your sketches, the less it matters how they look in other respects. The important thing is that your sketches communicate the essential information about your concept to the person viewing them.

CREATE COMPS BASED ON THE BEST ROUGH SKETCHES

Years ago, I learned to make comps by combining printed and drawn type with printed and drawn images. The process was akin to making a collage, though much more precise. Now, comps are usually created on the computer. Comps are arguably the graphic designer's equivalent of the architect's scale model or the sculptor's maquette. They present a realistic depiction of a finished product but cost less in terms of time, effort, and money than a finished product.

We'll discuss how to create the responsive designer's equivalent to traditional comps—the web-based mockup—in the next chapter.

Sketching on devices

Since we're talking about responsive design, I recommend doing some of your rough sketching on actual devices (**Figure 7.3**). There are plenty of apps (including free ones) that will turn your tablet or smartphone into a blank canvas, ready for you to sketch your UI ideas and export them as images that

Figure 7.3
Sketching on device screens encourages extra consideration of the size and spacing of on-screen elements. (Photo courtesy of Travis Holmes)

you can then import into the image editor of your choice (or straight into a web mockup) as a guide for creating more detailed comps. Sketching on devices lets you explore the size of elements (is that button too small?), as well as color and general layout. More importantly, it allows you to do this *very quickly*.

For quite a while I drew with my finger on various devices. Then Stephanie Rieger recommended that I use a touchscreen stylus, so I could actually *draw* on the screen like I would draw on paper. Boy, did I feel stupid for not thinking of that one. Luckily, the advantages of using a stylus quickly made up for my feelings of inadequacy and I'm no longer in therapy. Buy a touchscreen stylus if you don't have one.

The great thing about these sketches is that you can export them and use them as a background in whatever application you use for fleshing out your designs (**Figure 7.4**). I like to set a sketch as a background image to a web page with CSS, which gives me a starting point for setting up a layout grid and considering potential changes in that grid depending on screen size. If you've paid attention to the size of the elements in your sketches (such as the size of buttons), setting a background image in this way helps to ensure that what you create in your mockup HTML/CSS will be similar to your original sketches.

Figure 7.4
Sketches can be used as a guide for creating more detailed mockups.

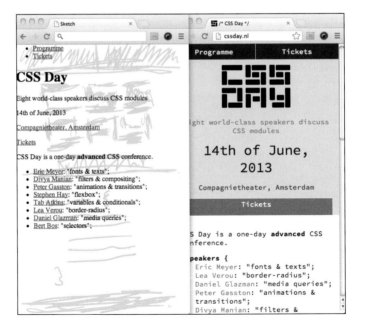

Figure 7.5
Sketching advocates like Mike Rohde encourage sketching as an aid to thinking. (Image courtesy of Mike Rohde)

Sketching as a habit

Proponents of sketching often advocate turning sketching into a habit. For some, like Mike Rohde, author of *The Sketchnote Handbook*, it's become a way of life (**Figure 7.5**).[3] Rohde gives us an answer to the *why* of sketching in *Sketching: The Visual Thinking Power Tool*, an article he wrote for *A List Apart:*[4]

"Adding sketching to the design process is a great way to amplify software and hardware tools. Sketching provides a unique space that can help you think differently, generate a variety of ideas quickly, explore alternatives with less risk, and encourage constructive discussions with colleagues and clients." — MIKE ROHDE

---

3 Mike Rohde, *The Sketchnote Handbook* (Peachpit Press, 2012).

4 Mike Rohde, "Sketching: the Visual Thinking Power Tool." *A List Apart.* http://www.alistapart.com/articles/sketching-the-visual-thinking-power-tool/.

He also stresses the importance of the sketch as a *thinking tool* as opposed to a work of art. "Ugly gets the job done just fine," he says.

While Rohde and other sketch artists like Danny Gregory use sketching as others might use a diary, that's not necessarily the way you have to do it. Even Gregory fell out of the sketching habit for a while after becoming a father and author. But you *can* turn sketching into a habit for your web design work, a way to help you think about various possibilities and explore design ideas before jumping on the computer.

Try it out!

Only sweat the major breakpoints (for now)

As mentioned earlier, Jeremy Keith notes that what happens between the breakpoints is just as important as the breakpoints themselves—perhaps even more so. While I agree with this, we do have to start somewhere. In a way, this part of the process reminds me of storyboarding, or creating animation keyframes, with the in-between frames being developed later. We're going to do that here.

Major break-points are conditions that, when met, trigger major changes in your design. A major breakpoint might be, for example, where your entire layout must change from two columns to four.

Let's say you've chosen three basic design directions from your thumbnails. Think about what your **major breakpoints** will look like (**Figure 7.6**). And here's the key: *try to come up with as few major breakpoints as possible.* That might sound crazy, since we're talking about responsive design. After all, we have media queries, so let's use about 12 of them, right? No! If a linear layout works for every screen and is *appropriate* for your particular concept, then there's no need for different layouts. In that case, simply describe what will happen when the screen gets larger. Will everything generally stay the same, with changes only to font size, line height and margins? If so, sketch those. For these variations, make thumbnails first, explore some options, and then move on to larger, more detailed sketches. Use your breakpoint graph as a guide at first and make sketches according to the breakpoints you've estimated on your graph.

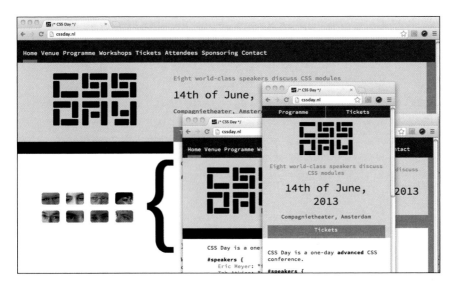

Figure 7.6
Most websites need very few major breakpoints.

When thinking about major breakpoints, remember to think about *device classes*. If you're thinking about smartphones, tablets, laptops/desktops, TVs, and game consoles, for example, you're heading in the right direction. If you're thinking in terms of brand names and specific operating systems, you're on the wrong track. The idea is to think in terms of general device classifications and, sometimes, device capabilities. Capabilities are more important when designing web applications, since you should be thinking about what screens will look like both with and *without* any particular capability.

Rough sketches of major breakpoints can help you determine:

* Whether or not more major breakpoints are needed

* Which design choice will be the most labor intensive; you might opt for a design that will better fit within time and budget constraints

* Whether or not a particular device class has been neglected or needs further consideration

* What technologies you'll need to develop the design responsively

Rough sketches are more detailed than thumbnails, but they shouldn't take a long time to create. In a short period, you should have a sketch of each major breakpoint for each of your chosen designs. This should be enough to decide on one of the designs.

Minor break-points are conditions that, when met, trigger small changes in your design. An example would be moving form labels from above text fields to the left of those fields, while the rest of the design remains the same.

So where and when will you sketch **minor breakpoints**? *In the browser*, when you do your web-based mockup. You'll find out why and how in the next chapter. In the meantime, simply focus on making sketches of the state of your web pages or app screens at the major breakpoints of each design.

At this point, don't worry too much if you notice that the initial breakpoints on your breakpoint graph simply won't do. Those were just a starting point, and you're free to revise your estimate based on your sketches. You might even decide that you need an extra breakpoint for a given design and record that in sketch form; you can add that breakpoint to your graph. This is a cycle of discovery, learning, and revision.

Think about your content while sketching

While sketching, you'll certainly be thinking about the way things should look. My experience is that much UI sketching of this type revolves around the layout of elements on the screen. I've found it useful to keep thinking about the content while sketching, and to consider what will happen to the content in various situations. When designing responsively, it can be useful to consider how you'll handle the following content in particular:

◆ Text

◆ Navigation

◆ Tables

Oh, sure, there are many more things to consider, and you'll end up creating your own list of "things to do some extra thinking about" as the project progresses. For now, let's take a look at the items listed above.

Text

Before you say, "Hey, wait a minute, didn't you just tell me that I didn't have to draw text while sketching?" hear me out. While sketching, there are a couple of text-related issues you'll need to tackle: column width and text size, both of which are relevant *in proportion to the screen and the other elements on the page.*

Column width is fairly obvious, but it can be difficult to estimate how wide a column will be with *actual text*. In this case, sketching on a device might give you a better idea of the actual space you have to work with. Another method I've used is just to make a simple HTML page that contains only text, and load that into a device's browser (or even an emulator, which while not optimal still gives a more realistic impression than lines on paper). When the text seems too large or too small, you can adjust the font size accordingly. Once it seems right, you'll be able to make your sketches a bit more realistic.

Think about the size of links—not only the text size, but also the amount of space around them. Both of these factors play a role in the touchability or clickability of links (and buttons): large links and buttons are easier targets, but slightly smaller links with plenty of space around them can work just as well. That said, there's a decent chance that no matter what you choose to sketch, you'll end up making changes again when you create your mockups.

This is the great thing about sketching that I can't repeat often enough: you're going to refine your design in the browser anyway, so the speed with which you can try things out when sketching means you won't have to do detail work more than once (unless your client has changes, but we all know that never happens).

Navigation

Navigation is another poster child for sketching on actual devices. The size issues are the same as with links, but there's a lot more thinking to do in terms of the design of navigation for various devices, which means navigation might change significantly at each major breakpoint.

Think back to Bryan Rieger's practice of designing in text first, and ponder what you would do *before* the very first breakpoint if you had only plain HTML and CSS at your disposal—in other words, if you had no JavaScript. That means no,

NOTE

Distinguish between touchability and clickability. Many designers, myself included, have made the mistake of refining links for people who click on them using a mouse, or even via the keyboard, without considering how touchable these links are for people on touch devices.

you can't have your menu collapsed at the top of the screen and have it drop down when someone touches it. If you have your menu at the top, it's in its expanded form and takes up all the vertical space it normally would.

This is a controversial enough subject, with even accessibility gurus in disagreement: JavaScript, after all, is currently considered an "accessibility supported" technology. But this isn't necessarily about accessibility. It's about *thinking* about what happens when a browser lacks JavaScript support, or if the JavaScript available on the device is different than what you'd expect. Your content will be presented in a certain way before JavaScript does its thing with it, no matter what the browser. So why not think about what that initial state will be?

In the chapter on wireframes, I talked about my preferred pattern for navigation on the smallest screens: keep it near the bottom of the screen and place a link to that navigation near the top of the screen. JavaScript, when available and working as expected, can move that navigation up to the top and create the drop-down menu on the fly.

But a pattern is not design law, so how you choose to handle the smallest screens will depend on your project. If I had only a few links in my navigation, I might very well put the menu at the top from the very start, and there it would stay at every breakpoint.

Remember that JavaScript and CSS let you do a lot of rearranging of stuff on the screen. That knowledge should empower you to safely design a great page with plain HTML and use JavaScript and CSS to spice it up any way you like. This is the essence of progressive enhancement.

Tables

Tables! Oh, the bane of the responsive designer (or wait, is that images? Or video? Or layout? Ahem). Tables are tough to deal with on small screens. I'd love to tell you I have all the answers, but instead I have more questions. Hopefully, these will lead you to a solution. It's good to think about these while you're sketching.

First of all, what types of tables will you be dealing with? Narrow? Wide? Numerical? Textual? Your content inventory should give you enough information to answer these simple questions. Once you've considered those, try to categorize the types of tables you have into something like the following classes (**Figure 7.7**):

◆ **Small-screen-friendly tables,** which you'll probably leave as they are, because they're small enough and will work fine on most small screens.

◆ **Blockable tables,** which you can alter with CSS so that each row in the table functions visually as a block item in a list (**Figure 7.8**).

◆ **Chartable tables,** which contain numerical data that can be transformed into a chart, graph, or other visualization that will take up less space on a small screen.

◆ **Difficult tables,** which are hard enough to deal with that you'll need to come up with a different plan for them, sometimes even on a case-by-case basis. These are our enemies, but unfortunately, are the friends of our clients, who all love Microsoft Excel. Oh well.

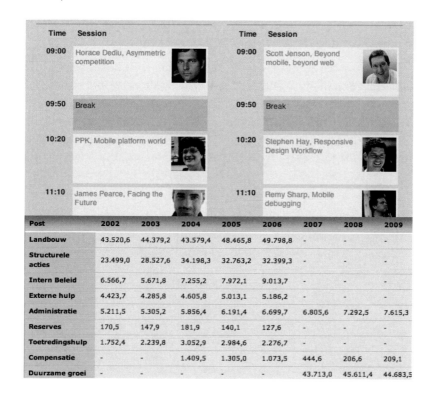

Figure 7.7
There are several different types of tables, and different ways of dealing with them on small screens. (Sources: mobilism. nl and eu-verant-woording.nl)

Figure 7.8
One way of dealing with small screen tables is to treat each row as a block.

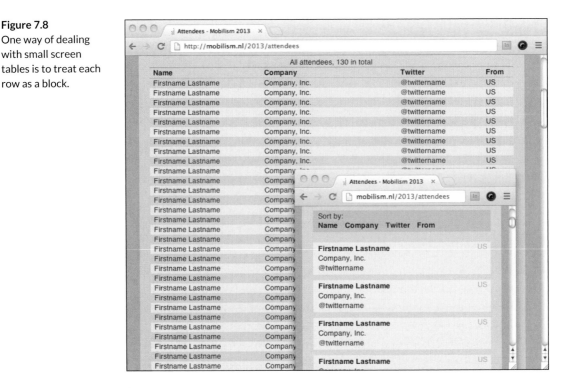

Thinking again in terms of progressive enhancement, the base design should probably just include the whole table, which means that the user will have to scroll horizontally to see the whole thing in many cases. On top of this, we can employ CSS and JavaScript, when they're available, to do some magic for us. Blockable and chartable tables can be *blocked* with CSS and *charted* with JavaScript. Plenty of designers and developers have experimented with many different options for tables, from simply making the table itself scrollable to exchanging columns and rows.

The fun part is that what you do on small screens isn't necessarily what you'll do on larger screens. That's why now—when all you have to do is sketch and it won't take much time—is the time to think about the changes you'll be making at each breakpoint.

What to do if you get stuck

Every designer gets stuck at some point. It's no big deal unless you treat it like one. There are countless ways to deal with it, from asking yourself *what if* questions ("What if it weren't a table, but a list?" is what I asked myself before "blockifying" the attendees table for the Mobilism site) to the cliché *taking a shower*, which you hopefully do on a regular basis anyway. The reason this chapter focuses so much on sketching is because the act of drawing itself can actually stimulate your brain to come up with more ideas, provided you push it hard enough by sketching past your comfort zone of first-come ideas.

If your problem is that you're stuck creatively, there are many inspiring books and resources to get your creative engine started during the bitter cold of designer's block. Although there are plenty of resources on design and creativity itself (try such classics as Edward de Bono's *Lateral Thinking*), the greatest inspiration can come from sources outside the realm of design.[5] Trying to combine things that normally aren't combined can lead to surprising results. It's a simple little trick, but I've often used Brian Eno and Peter Schmidt's *Oblique Strategies* to force me to take a different approach.[6] Worst case, it's a lot of fun. Best case, you've got a great idea!

If your problem is that you're not sure how to handle something in the context of responsive design, there's no harm in researching how others have solved problems like yours. Just be sure to use your creativity and tailor any ideas you might find to your own situation; after all, you're a designer. At the time of this writing I find Brad Frost's *This Is Responsive* to be one of the most exhaustive collections of responsive design patterns and resources available.[7] You can spend hours going through there and you'll certainly come across something that will get you unstuck.

So anyway, are you done sketching your design? Great! Relax, that was the hard part. Um, oh wait. (Just kidding, relax. In the next chapter, you get to do some coding.)

---

5 Edward de Bono, *Lateral Thinking* (Viking, 2009).
6 http://en.wikipedia.org/wiki/Oblique_Strategies
7 http://bradfrost.github.com/this-is-responsive/

## 8

CREATING A WEB-BASED DESIGN MOCKUP

"My name is web design, and I have a problem."
—STEPHANIE RIEGER

NOTE

A great advantage of using web-based mockups is that while viewing them in the browser, you can open up your browser's developer tools and make changes on the fly. This is great for trying out ideas.

By now my opinion on static mockups should be clear: they're not practical for responsive design. They're not effectively scalable. Once you have a static mockup, creating a second doesn't double work time, but both time and cost *will be increased*—all the more as multiples increase. Many changes have to be made manually, which is ridiculous when we have technology that can make it easier for us.

Imagine being asked by a client to change the font sizes of all your headings. To do this in a Photoshop document, you'd have to bump up the size of every single heading, and adjust the margins and spacing around them. You might also have to change the placement of other text or images to accommodate the new heading sizes and make the document bigger so everything will fit. Now imagine that when you've finished making those changes, you still need to make the same changes for the mobile and tablet versions.

Now picture opening a CSS file, changing one or two style rules for headings, saving that file, and opening up a single web page in your browser to see the changes immediately. Imagine opening that same page on a smartphone

EVOLUTION

We could call these mockups *evolutionary prototypes*, if we're willing to create our wireframes responsively with web technology and gradually evolve them into full-blown design prototypes. This process may take some getting used to, but it works on real projects extremely well. This way of working can save an incredible amount of time and the advantages are plenty. Consider the design of interactions, such as hovers or how elements look when they receive focus. These don't need to be described or visualized in a separate layer in static documents; they can simply be demonstrated live. Consider state changes such as "logged in" or "logged out," which may influence some aspects of the design. With a trivial bit of code, you can toggle these state changes on and off in the browser, which is ideal for showing clients and developers how things should look and behave.

The implications of this are potentially tremendous. The combination of various disciplines such as visual design, interaction design, and front-end development can be put into a working prototype. Not so with static mockups.

and magically seeing those changes applied to the mobile design. That alone makes the case for using web-based mockups for responsive web design, as opposed to image editor files. If you choose to journey down this path, you'll find that there are many more advantages.

Throughout this book, you've been preparing to create a web-based mockup. You got representative content into the browser as early as possible. You created (responsive!) wireframes in the browser. You created a working linear design in the browser. And you sketched and developed ideas for your design at various breakpoints. Now you're ready, at least materially, to combine these efforts into a working prototype. Once you have your prototype, you'll further visualize the sketches you made in the previous chapter with CSS. From that point on, *all your design revisions will be done in the browser*. Changes will be tracked with version control. You can still be creative, sketching any changes you might want to make before implementing them with CSS. But you'll have the reality check of viewing in actual browsers. You'll be able to utilize time-saving developer tools. You'll be setting the stage for the creation of auto-updating design documentation (which we'll discuss later). Most importantly, you'll keep your sanity when changes come.

NOTE

Web-based mockups are, in effect, prototypes of web pages or screens, since they're in the browser. To emphasize that fact, I use the terms mockup and prototype interchangeably in this chapter.

Hurdles to acceptance

As with any change, there's work to be done to make everyone on the project comfortable with a new way of working. Results may be convincing, but those tend to come later in the process.

Clients (generally) don't care

Clients don't care what tools you use, as long as you get the job done. They probably won't see the difference between an image from Photoshop or a screenshot from a browser, except for the fact that the latter will most likely be more realistic, since it's what the design *actually looks like in the browser*. No more selling clients pretty pictures now and making concessions later. No more annoying surprises for clients and frustrating discussions about differences between what the browser renders and what the client signed off on.

"Demonstrating our designs to clients as XHTML/CSS pages rather than as static Photoshop or Fireworks has streamlined our workflow and helped us to set and manage a client's expectations better than ever before." —ANDY CLARKE[1]

This all sounds great, but you'll probably still encounter some hurdles when you do web-based mockups—at least until they become the norm. As always, the biggest problems are people problems, and people with an aversion to this approach can cause you some frustration.

There are two types of people, other than clients, whose aversion might make this approach challenging:

1. Other people

2. You

Let's examine the problems with both.

Other people

Other people—project managers, developers, and the like—might be uncomfortable with tossing old-school, waterfall-based deliverables in favor of new-school, iterative deliverables. After all, some people expect to see details worked out in wireframes before anything is built. Some developers are afraid of anyone else doing HTML and CSS, even if they don't have to use it.

Not long ago, I was hired to lead the design of a large, information-rich government website. Another company was responsible for implementing the content management system and translating the design to HTML/CSS templates. They requested Photoshop templates. I said no (I have to say that

---

1 Andy Clarke, "Time to stop showing clients static design visuals | Stuff & Nonsense," Stuff & Nonsense, september 22, 2008, http://www.stuffandnonsense.co.uk/blog/about/time_to_stop_showing_clients_static_design_visuals/.

a lot); they would be getting web-based prototypes in HTML and CSS, with a tiny bit of JavaScript. They had trouble dealing with the idea, and our conversation went something like this:

"That will take more time to do; we can't use your markup and CSS. Our CMS outputs different markup."

"You don't have to use my markup. I use it to create the prototype. I'm not creating the templates. You're free to do those as you please."

"But it's more work for us."

"How, exactly? How do you normally go from Photoshop to HTML and CSS?"

"We measure everything and we slice out images as necessary."

Slicing. Old school. So, as most front-end developers probably work today, they're using the eyedropper to get color values, the ruler for measuring margins. They're selecting text and studying the values in the text palette to get the values they need for their CSS.

"So I'm giving you the images you need, web-ready, and I'm giving you CSS which has the values you need right there. How does that create more work for you?"

"Well, okay, it's probably not more work. But it's not less work either."

NOTE

If the client or developer is absolutely set on getting images as a deliverable instead of web-based mockups, you can always take screenshots of the mockups and deliver the screenshots (see Chapter 9, "Presentation, Round One: Screenshots"). You'll be able to provide image assets, but no Photoshop files.

"BUILDING" SOUNDS EXPENSIVE

The fact that web-based mockups are viewable in the browser might give some the impression that it's already built in whole or in part, rather than a depiction (created with web technology) of what *will* be built later on. This is most likely because the design is built with the same technology that will be used to build the actual site.

This is a potential hurdle you'll need to overcome in order to keep clients from thinking you're "almost done" and that development should be easier since you're so far along; this, as you can probably guess, isn't always the case. Changes in the *design* are quicker to do, but your work on a web-based mockup may or may not affect production time.

The fact that clients tend to have the impression that a web-based mockup is the actual website in an early stage is one of the reasons I choose to show screenshots of the mockup during the first design presentation. We'll discuss this more in Chapter 9.

Fair enough. I've had this discussion with several developers over the past couple of years. These are web professionals who probably do their work well. They're also resistant to change, which is logical. The fact is that once they get used to these deliverables, they *will* save time. It's a matter of practice. At least they were willing to go along with the process. That's the important thing—daring to try something new that might help improve things.

You

While other people might be an obstacle to trying something new, I regularly come across designers and developers who are pretty terrified of the process. They're the web designer equivalent of a kid who's never eaten salad declaring that she doesn't like salad. You know what happens? *They all end up loving salad* (cough).

If you're a visual or interaction designer with little or no coding experience, it's possible that this book has freaked you somewhat. To be clear: I'm asking you to learn HTML and CSS and to use these as design tools in much the same way you learned to use vector drawing applications or image editors such as Photoshop or GIMP (**Figure 8.1**). I've already asked you to use a plain text editor and some simple, easy-to-write commands in your computer's terminal emulator, a.k.a. the dreaded command line. You've recovered, haven't you?

Figure 8.1
Image editors (like GIMP, in this case) are quite complex applications.

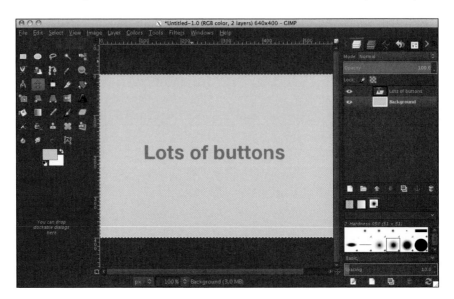

To some, this is hellishly scary. After all, you're "not technical." You're creative. *Not technical*? Really? Remember Photoshop and all those palettes, options, and buttons that look like Darth Vader's bathroom? Photoshop is an incredibly powerful application. You probably know how to adjust color through Levels and Curves. You work with layout grids and manipulate objects across layers and edit colors through channels. You have tricks for creating things like special borders and shadows that you could otherwise create with one or two lines of CSS. You may know about color spaces and color theory. In fact, there's a whole book about the Photoshop LAB color space—a whole book. And basic HTML and CSS is too technical? Come on. Print designers know about ink and paper and things like dot gain. They do technical preflight checks on the documents they send to the printer. You could memorize the most common HTML elements in less than an hour and learn basic CSS styling in another. It can take you days to get your head around the interface of a complex image manipulation program like Photoshop, and months or years to master it.

Admittedly, advanced HTML and CSS will also take years to master, and they are now (officially) changing all the time. But that's what web designs are made of, so the more you know, the better you'll get at applying your design ideas to the web. They're like any other tool, or even a musical instrument. You want to get to the point that you're no longer thinking to make the notes; you just want to focus on the nuances of the piece you're playing. That takes a long time. That said, I can guarantee you that learning HTML and CSS (if you don't already know them)—and perhaps even some JavaScript—will almost never be a waste of time. As with anything, the more you know about how the web is made, the more you'll be able to create a mental map of what's possible, the more you'll be able to educate your clients and stakeholders, and the less time you'll spend revising things in layered pictures across tens or hundreds of documents.

My point is this: don't doubt your abilities. You're technical enough. You're smart enough. Nobody's asking you to be a programmer. If you learned Photoshop, you can learn basic HTML and CSS. And you'll learn to love what you can do with them, *in addition* to Photoshop.

After learning to create mockups in the form of HTML and CSS prototypes, you'll see that using Photoshop for creating image assets and playing around with ideas frees your creative mind. You can think creatively and use your newfound knowledge to test your visual hypotheses in the browser, the *actual medium in which your work will be published*. That's an incredible opportunity that's absolutely unique to web design.

Of course, if you're a weird sort of hybrid designer-developer type like me, you might be quick to warm up to the idea of web technologies as design tools.

Presenting your mockups

Presenting designs to clients (and others) is an art form. It involves the ability to read or infer what others are thinking by looking for the right clues, and taking steps to emphasize the effectiveness of the design and address or alleviate any concerns your client might have.

I often call the processes and methods around client presentations *presentation psychology*. One of the key issues when presenting web-based prototypes is the very real risk that the client will get the impression that you're further along in the design or development process than you actually are.

We'll discuss presenting in detail, including how to overcome this common obstacle, in Chapter 9, "Presentation, Round One: Screenshots," and Chapter 10, "Presentation, Round Two: In the Browser." First, let's go through the process of developing a web-based mockup.

Let's get to work

To create web-based design mockups, there are a few things you'll need:

- A text editor (not to be confused with a word processor).
- A modern web browser
- Some basic knowledge of HTML and CSS (JavaScript knowledge is a plus but not essential) or access to a friendly front-end developer who's willing to help you out.

NOTE
Remember, my goal is to recommend tools that are free to use and easy to acquire, so that anyone with a computer and web access can use them. There's much you can create without spending a dime!

In this chapter, you'll also learn about software that can help you create prototypes more quickly and easily, and which admittedly has a learning curve: a **static site generator**. I'm using Dexy (which is in fact not a static site generator, but documentation software that has that functionality) for the examples in this book, but there are many different static site generators available using many different programming languages.[2]

Of course, there are many other tools you can use, especially if you're a bit more technically inclined, such as CSS preprocessors. Preprocessors like Sass or LESS can greatly speed up your prototyping work. Use of preprocessors is optional. However, they can provide you with a massive speed increase and thus are well worth the effort involved in learning them.

A **static site generator** lets you create content in separate documents, from which you can generate a website that doesn't require a content management system.

Evolving your responsive wireframe

Now it's time to dust off the content reference wireframes we made in Chapter 3, "Content Reference Wireframes," and morph them into static prototypes. The wireframes aren't much more than boxes within a layout. They already have a responsive base, which makes our job a bit easier.

When we made the wireframes in Chapter 3, our purpose wasn't necessarily to create a finished layout. Our goal was to prioritize content and illustrate a general idea of where things *could* be placed on the screen. In Chapter 7, "Designing for Breakpoints," we actually sketched out the design and you might even have put together some mood boards, made some studies in an image editor like Photoshop, or created some image assets.

The design thinking determines what we'll visualize via mockups. The wireframes, however, might give us a good starting point for the base HTML.

The first thing to do is compare the basic page layout of our design from Chapter 7 with your original wireframes. The idea isn't to look at the layout of components, but rather the building blocks of the page: things like the header, the footer, the main content area, and any other large blocks or columns. Are your design sketches different from your wireframes? Note the differences so you have a list of things you'll need to change.

TIP

It might be good to start with something other than the home page. Many websites and applications have one layout that's used for the majority of pages or screens. Try to find that particular design and the corresponding wireframe and compare them.

---

2 http://www.dexy.it

If the building blocks are basically the same, you're good to go. If not, you'll need to adjust the HTML of the wireframes to fit the newest version of your design. In our book site, we don't have to change the actual structure of the HTML, though we'll certainly be changing the CSS to fit the design.

The process of developing a mockup from this point is straightforward:

1. Copy the various pieces of content from your linear design and paste them into the correct containers in the wireframe; save this as a new HTML file so you don't accidentally overwrite your wireframe (but save it in the same folder so it still points to the right style sheets). If you look at this file in a browser, you'll see a combination of your wireframe with your linear design, only without much style.

2. Remove the `wireframe` class from the `body` element.

3. Adjust the CSS so the elements on the page correspond to your newest design.

These steps aren't always trivial (especially the last one), but when you've finished you'll have a working, web-based mockup of your design for narrow viewports. During this process, you should constantly be looking at your page in real browsers, preferably several different ones. If you can do this on different platforms and different devices, even better. Repeat this process for every page type you want to include in your design. Simple, right?

It's not fair of me to gloss over point three, "adjust the CSS," like that, is it? It's the most involved, so let's look at that step in more detail.

ADDING STYLE

Unless you came up with totally different typographical style ideas in Chapter 7, your linear design styles are a good place to start shaping your CSS. Remember `base.css`? Copy all the styles from your linear design and paste them into `base.css` under your wireframe styles.

NOTE

Theoretically, you could remove the wireframe styles now if you like. I usually leave them in and re-move them when I'm completely finished with the mockup.

The rest comes down to sculpting your CSS so that your page, when viewed in a narrow viewport, matches your vision of how that should look. Start with mobile first: open the design on a smartphone or an emulator (or your desktop browser with a narrow window) and look at the page. Work as quickly as you can, editing your HTML file to adjust structure, content, and attributes like `class` and `id` as needed. Work only in `base.css` for style, unless you prefer to use a preprocessor.

Don't fall into the trap of feeling that you have to develop a complete, working static website just because you're working with HTML and CSS. This is one of the arguments used against designing in the browser, but if you work efficiently, you should be able to work just as quickly, if not more quickly, than you would in Photoshop.

Once you've completed the "mobile" version of this page, start expanding your browser window until something doesn't look right. It could be that your main text column is less readable because it contains too many characters, or perhaps your logo looks too small compared to the rest of the page. Form input fields might become too wide for your taste. When you get to one of these points, stop. It's time for a breakpoint.

HOW PERFECT DOES THE HTML NEED TO BE?

This depends on what lies in store for your files. Will they be used only to convey the design, or will they be used for development?

If you're both the designer and the front-end developer and you'd like to have the mockups become the actual front-end templates for development, you'll end up paying more attention to the sectioning elements you choose, such as `<section>` and `<article>` versus simple `<div>` elements. You'll also want to pay close attention to your CSS, since you'll want to keep it as concise as possible. These are good habits to get into anyway, but they're especially important if your mockups will end up becoming a base for production.

If you're "only" the visual designer and someone else will be creating code based on your design, don't worry too much about code form. While best practices in front-end code are useful to follow, you're simply using a tool other than Photoshop to visualize a design. If you had visualized the design in Photoshop, there would be *no code at all*. Take the pressure off yourself and see this process as simply a more effective way of creating a picture of the design for your client. Follow best practices and be as semantic as you like with your HTML, as long as it doesn't slow you down. Your goal at this point is to visualize the design, nothing more.

WHIP OUT YOUR BREAKPOINT GRAPH

Most browsers come with **developer tools** built in; some you can install as extensions (such as the well-known Firebug). They let you inspect the elements on a page, alter CSS and HTML, debug JavaScript, and much, much more. Check your browser's documentation.

If you've been working through the chapters with me, you estimated what your breakpoints would be on a breakpoint graph. Now's the time to see if your estimates were correct. Open your browser's **developer tools**/web inspector and look at the "computed styles" (**Figure 8.2**). Find the width of the html element. Compare this value to the value of the first breakpoint on your breakpoint graph. It may or may not be close to your estimate. It doesn't matter.

The breakpoint graph contains estimates of where we would put our breakpoints. I didn't really expect the estimates to be totally accurate; they were useful just to get us thinking about what changes we might make. What we've done at this point is expanded the viewport to the point that our layout "breaks" and found out how wide the viewport is by looking at the computed styles. Play with your browser window a bit and choose a point *just before* the point where your design breaks. Now replace the estimate for the first breakpoint on your graph with this new value. This transforms the breakpoint graph from an estimate into part of your design *documentation* (more on that in Chapter 11, "Creating Design Guidelines"). It also means that we're setting breakpoints based on what the *designed content* is doing, which is a good thing.

Figure 8.2
The Computed Styles view in your browser's developer tools lets you see how the browser actually applies your CSS.

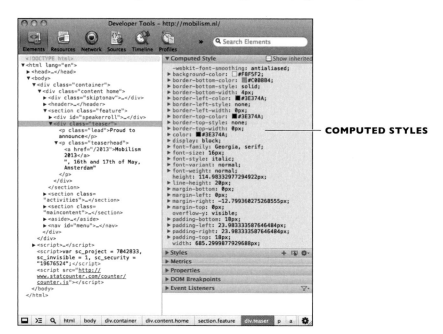

Now that you know what that first breakpoint is and have changed your breakpoint graph accordingly, you can also change the `min-width` value of your first breakpoint in the HTML:

```
<link rel="stylesheet" href="styles/medium.css"
→media="only screen and (min-width: [your breakpoint])">
```

Since `medium.css` will contain the styles we use between this breakpoint and the next, you can start adding CSS to that file. Try to think in terms of "additive CSS," building up from the basic styles you already have (a form of progressive enhancement). In fact, you use this file to describe the style *exceptions* compared to `base.css`. I often use `base.css` for all styles that need to be applied to a given site *regardless of the layout* and as such it's relatively larger, while `medium.css` contains predominantly layout changes and is usually smaller. `large.css` is often the smallest.

Thus many of the changes in `medium.css` will be changes in the positioning and size of elements. Margins might get wider, padding may be adjusted, and the menu might be moved to the top of the screen from its original home at the bottom of the page. One column might become two. Elements that were originally positioned vertically might now be positioned horizontally. Remember the first tenet of responsive design and keep to a fluid layout grid, using relative units so your design can expand sufficiently. When you're finished, your page should look like what you designed for your first breakpoint.

TACKLING THE REMAINING MAJOR BREAKPOINTS

In many cases, you'll need only three major breakpoints. I've never had to use more than four. However many you use, you'll simply repeat the process described above for each of them:

1. Expand the browser window until the design no longer works.

2. Adjust the window to the point just before that breakpoint.

3. Note the viewport width.

4. Replace the value in both your breakpoint graph and the `link` element in your HTML.

5. Add and adjust styles in the relevant style sheet until the page matches your design for that breakpoint.

TIP

The Computed Style view in your browser's developer tools is useful for multiplatform design. As opposed to the regular Style view, which shows the CSS as it should be applied to the page, Computed Style shows the styles as interpreted by the browser. Check this when you want to see why something looks the way it does in a given browser.

NOTE

There are plenty of ways to see how wide your viewport is, from browser extensions specifically for that purpose, to writing your own JavaScript to print the current viewport width on your page.

Meanwhile, keep seeing each breakpoint as a *range*, rather than as a frozen image. If your first breakpoint is at 400px and your second at 900px, then you design for the first breakpoint is what people will experience in any situation where they view your site *between 400px and 900px*. That's why fluid layout is so important: the page needs to "feel" right throughout that entire range, not only at 400px and 900px.

SPEEDING THINGS UP

Here are a few tips to help speed things up:

1.   Use a CSS preprocessor. It's a tremendous time-saver to not have to worry about remembering often-used colors and styles you've applied to certain components. Variables will help you in that department. CSS preprocessors also remove practically any effort you might otherwise have in calculating things like margins.

2.   Use a static site generator or similar templating system. A static site generator lets you put elements common to all pages (such as headers and footers) into a common template and keep only the content for your prototype pages in separate files. Not only will changes in the common elements be instantly available in all your pages, but some static site generators will actually accept Markdown for content, so you never even have to dive (much) into HTML unless you choose to.

3.   Don't worry about browser compatibility. Again, these prototypes are replacements for Photoshop mockups. The first time you show them to the client, you could even show screenshots instead of showing the design in the browser. More on that in Chapter 9. Just make sure your design works in a modern, easy-to-acquire web browser, perhaps even a browser your client might have. You'll eventually show your client how the design looks on mobile, though, so at the time of this writing I'd recommend choosing a browser with solid mobile versions, such as Firefox, Chrome, or Opera.

4.   Don't sweat all the details. Unless your client signs off on something like style tiles, you'll want to avoid obsessing for hours about the exact gradient on that button. It's important that your prototype depicts your design accurately, but use your good judgment when considering how far you go with the details. Show clients proportions, not pixels.

From static page to static site generator

You can create each mockup page by hand if you like, going through the above process. Each mockup will be a separate HTML file, each containing its own header and footer, each linking to the appropriate assets such as style sheets and images. All of your content, real and simulated, will be hard-coded in HTML.

For one or two mockups, this is just fine. For more (and many projects need more), this process doesn't offer a significant increase in speed or maintainability compared to Photoshop comps. It does offer the important benefits of responsiveness and realism, but we have an opportunity to increase the benefit of web-based mockups by using a static site generator.

Static site generators (SSGs) are software applications that generate a website from a series of files. There are many types of SSGs, from the bare-bones variety for very simple sites to full-featured apps that offer things like tagging and archives for blogs. There are SSGs in practically every commonly used programming language (and each language has several to choose from). Nanoc, a popular SSG, maintains quite a large list of SSGs for various languages on its website (they're obviously not afraid of the competition).[3] However, a quick web search will uncover many more options.

One factor that should influence your decision is the choice of templating language.

Templating

A templating language in this context is a language (however small) that lets you create *templates*. Templates, in turn, allow you to insert placeholders for other content. Take the following sentence as an example:

```
The book will be called {{title}}.
```

In this sentence, the templating language I'm using is called Jinja, and `{{title}}` is a variable. The idea is that the templating system will replace the variable with the content it represents. In this case, that is the title of the book.

---

3 http://nanoc.stoneship.org/docs/1-introduction/#similar-projects

Templates can also contain logic, which can allow you, for example, to loop through a list of items in order to create an HTML list. You might use this logic at some point, but it does complicate things. Avoid logic in your templates until you feel completely comfortable with templating in general.

Many static site generators provide or work with existing templating systems. Templating is important, because it lets you use plain text markup on pieces of content and include those pieces of content in HTML documents via templates. This makes it easy for people to provide you with content, or for you to mock up your own and then edit it without wading through HTML. HTML isn't hard, but plain text markup is that much simpler.

When choosing a static site generator, you'll want to examine and make sure you like the templating system it uses.

Choosing an SSG

The SSG I currently use is the same software I use for creating style guides and other types of documentation. This was an important factor for me. Once you do a bit of research, you'll find factors that are important to you. Consider things like:

◆ Programming language: This is necessary if you want to extend your SSG's capabilities, and sometimes to write configuration files.

◆ Templating system/language: This is often tied to the SSG's programming language.

◆ Markup language(s): If you prefer Markdown and your SSG supports only reStructuredText,[4] you'll have to extend the SSG or find a different one.

◆ Configuration: Most SSGs use some sort of configuration file. Do you have to know a specific programming language to create one?

◆ Ease of use: Remember, this is just a tool, so you don't want to spend too much time fiddling around with it unless you get a huge return on that investment. Some tools are great but have little or difficult-to-understand documentation. If there are no other resources, you might base your decision in part on how quickly you can pick up the basics.

---

4 http://docutils.sourceforge.net/rst.html

If you're unfamiliar with SSGs, simply follow along with me, using the same software I use. You won't need any prior knowledge. Once you become comfortable with it, you can experiment with other software that fits your requirements (or you might decide to stick with this one!).

If you have a preferred SSG, you can follow along and execute similar steps using that software.

Be aware that we're going to recreate the above process of creating a web-based mockup, only now we're going to do that with the help of a static site generator. If you happened to code along with me earlier in this chapter, remember that in actual projects you'll either do static HTML mockups *or* use an SSG. You don't need to do both.

Introducing Dexy

The software I currently use for creating both mockups and documentation is called Dexy. Dexy is open-source software for documentation and automated documents. It just so happens that a static "website" is one of the document types that Dexy supports. This means that I don't have to use separate tools for mockups and style guides, which fits my own workflow nicely. Dexy is written in Python, which makes it easily available on many platforms. It also utilizes other useful software like Pygments for syntax highlighting of code (useful for style guides) and Jinja templates (useful for creating content placeholders in mockups and documentation).

Dexy is very young software and is in very active development at the time of this writing. You can think of it as software that takes files, does *stuff* with them, and then produces an output folder with the results of the "stuff it did." That "stuff" can be as simple as doing nothing at all, copying a file, putting it into a template, or piping it through other software and presenting the result. To do this stuff with files, Dexy provides *filters*. Dexy filters do things with files (or parts of them) on their own, or they can use other software to do this work. The filters then give back the result of what they executed. You can use this result in your documents. In some cases, the result might be a new file. Some examples might be appropriate here:

1. Take some Markdown files, inject each of them into a basic HTML template, and link the files together to create a simple website. (We'll be doing **that**!)

2. Take some CSS code snippets, insert them into some predefined placeholders in a Markdown file, and convert the file into HTML. And, oh yeah, give those code snippets some pretty colors in the final HTML file. (We'll be doing *that* too, in Chapter 11.)

3. Run some code in the command line, put the result of that command into a preexisting Markdown file, and then convert that to a PDF. Oh yeah, and Word, because your boss likes Word. (No, we'll skip that one.)

4. Visit the pages of a site in a browser and change the viewport size three times, taking a screenshot of certain elements in the page at each size. Put these screenshots into a preexisting Markdown document using templates, pull in syntax-highlighted CSS code that corresponds to each screenshot, and create an HTML page from all of that. (Yep, we'll be doing that as well when we make our style guide in Chapter 11.)

This is just the tip of the iceberg of what Dexy can do with its many filters (at the time of this writing, there are 135). And with each of the examples above, once you get everything set up (which can take a while), you'll simply type dexy in the command line and press Enter. Dexy will then do all the work for you. This makes changes easy.

If this sounds too technical already, breathe. Breathe in, breathe out—everything will be OK. I'll walk you through it—I promise. Since doing is learning and learning is doing, let's dive right in.

Installing Dexy

You already learned a bit about the command line a few chapters ago. That was the hard part. Installing Dexy is really easy, provided you have Python installed.

NOTE
If you don't have Python installed, you can find it at http://python.org/download/ and follow the installation instructions.

Python has a package manager called pip. To find out if you have it, type

```
$ pip install dexy
```

If you don't have the correct permissions on your system you may need to type sudo before this command and then enter your system password. If this works, you'll see that Dexy and its dependencies are being downloaded and installed. This can take a few minutes. The process is finished when you see a message like this:

```
Successfully installed dexy PyYAML chardet idiopidae jinja2
→mock nose ordereddict pexpect pygments python-modargs
→requests zapps
Cleaning up...
$
```

This message (or something similar claiming successful installation) should be followed by your command line prompt.

NOTE

Throughout these examples, the prompt is represented by a dollar ($) sign.

If so, congratulations! You just installed Dexy. To use some of the Dexy filters that rely on external software, you'll need to download and install that software as well. I'm assuming that by now you have Pandoc, so that's enough for right now. We'll install others later if necessary.

If you got an error doing `pip install dexy` because `pip` isn't on your system, you can type `easy_install pip` to install it, then try `pip install dexy` again. (Actually, you *can* do `easy_install dexy` and be done with it, but `pip` is pretty handy, and the more you do in the command line, the more comfortable you'll be).

NOTE

If you don't have Pandoc or think I'm referring to documents about cooking equipment, you might want to check out Chapter 5, "Linear Design."

Are you with me? Okay, let's make our mockup. We need an HTML skeleton, a navigation template, header and footer snippets, two configuration files, and a nice cup of coffee. To keep you sane, I'll provide you with everything but the coffee. First, install the base template I created for you:

```
$ pip install dexy_rdw
```

When that's complete, you can run:

```
$ dexy gen --t rdw:mockup --d [directory]
```

where `[directory]` is the name of the folder you want to create for your mockup. This folder will be created. Use `cd` to move into that folder once it's made. Now you'll see the following files and folders:

◆ `_base.html`
   This file contains the base HTML document with some Jinja templates for things like the `head` element, navigation, and main content template. You'll almost never need to touch this file.

◆ `_template.html`

   This is the main page template, which will pull in your main content from markdown files. Unless you're picky about the HTML element that holds your content, you won't need to touch this one either.

◆ `dexy.conf`

   This one tells Dexy to use its so-called "website reporter." Basically, it turns Dexy into a static site generator when we run dexy in this folder. There's no need to mess with this one.

◆ `dexy.yaml`

   You'll be spending some time in this file, which we'll discuss shortly. This file tells Dexy what to do to specific files when it's run. Here's where you tell Dexy which filters to run, and on which files.

◆ `index.markdown`

   You can consider this file to be the "home page" of your mockup. If your mockup is only one page, your content will go in this one. If your mockup is several pages, you'll have several Markdown documents, perhaps even in their own folders.

◆ `macros/_footer.html`

   This footer element will automatically be placed in every page in your mockup. You'll likely want to edit this one, but since it will show up on all pages, you only have to do it once.

◆ `macros/_head.html`

   This is the <head> element for all your pages. Here, we'll be linking to style sheets, as we did earlier in the <head> of our wireframes and linear design. Again, you need only do this once.

◆ `macros/nav.jinja`

   This consists of some Jinja macros that take advantage of Dexy's website reporter and automatically generate site navigation for us, based on the folders we use. You won't need to do anything with this file, which is called from _base.html. If you don't like or need the provided navigation, then simply remove the first line in _base.html that references it.

There. Aren't you glad all you had to do was provide the coffee?

Believe it or not, we already have a working web mockup, but none of our own content is in it yet. Type the following text in the command line:

```
$ dexy setup
```

This creates a couple of folders that Dexy uses to do its thing. Now simply run:

```
$ dexy
```

If you run `ls`, then you'll see that when Dexy was run, it created a couple of new folders. One of these is the `output-site` folder, and Dexy has created a basic mockup for us and put it in there. You could open the `index.html` file from that folder in your browser, but Dexy provides a simple web server to make things easier. Just run `dexy serve`. You'll see a message similar to this one:

```
serving contents of output-site on http://localhost:8085
type ctrl+c to stop
```

Open your browser to the URL in the message and you'll see the default mockup page (which has practically no content and uses no style sheets). It's not much, but it's a working static web page. You'll add your own content and style sheets (**Figure 8.3**). Go ahead and type CTRL-C in your terminal to stop the web server.

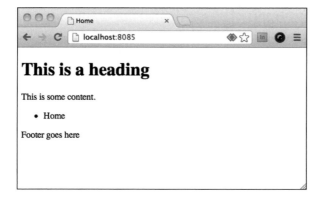

Figure 8.3
The default mockup template I've provided for you really needs *your* content.

Get your assets in here!

By now, you've created several deliverables:

- A content inventory

- At least one responsive content reference wireframe (and perhaps more)

- A linear design, which you converted from Markdown to HTML using Pandoc

- At least one breakpoint graph

- Sketches of what you'd like the site to look like at the various breakpoints

Since this mockup folder is new (it was created by Dexy when you ran dexy gen), we need to add assets like images and CSS to it. Copy your images folder (if you have one) and your *styles* folder from the project folder that contains your linear design and wireframes. In this mockup folder, you should now have *images* and *styles* folders in the same folder as dexy.yaml. If you have other assets, or folders you use if you use a CSS preprocessor, then you can copy them over them same way.

You can copy folders from the command line, if you like, by using cp -r.

Including style sheets

It's possible that you've already created the style sheets for your mockup. Whether or not you do, you'll still need to link to these files. Earlier I mentioned that the head part of your HTML is managed by the _head.html file, which is in the macros folder. Open that in a text editor:

```
<head>
    <meta charset="utf-8">
    <meta name="viewport"
    →content="width=device-width,initial-scale=1.0">
    {% if page_title == '' -%}
        <title>Home</title>
    {% else -%}
        <title>{{ page_title }}</title>
    {% endif %}
</head>
```

Now add the links to your style sheets:

```
<head>
    <meta charset="utf-8">
    <meta name="viewport"
    ➞content="width=device-width,initial-scale=1.0">
    {% if page_title == '' -%}
        <title>Home</title>
    {% else -%}
        <title>{{ page_title }}</title>
    {% endif %}
    <link rel="stylesheet" href="styles/base.css"
    ➞media="screen">
    <link rel="stylesheet" href="styles/medium.css"
    ➞media="only screen and (min-width: 600px)">
    <link rel="stylesheet" href="styles/large.css"
    ➞media="only screen and (min-width: 900px)">
</head>
```

TIP
Starting and stop-
ping dexy serve can
get annoying, so you
can open a second
terminal and simply
keep it running from
there, or if you're
more experienced
with command line
utilities, you can
use something like
GNU Screen.

Whenever you want to run Dexy again, you have to reset Dexy's cache. The easiest way to do that is by running dexy -r, which clears all the Dexy stuff from the current run, and then reruns Dexy. Try it now, followed again by dexy serve. Now refresh the page in your browser. The non-content is still there, but you should see that your styles have been applied (**Figure 8.4**).

Figure 8.4
The default mockup
now has your styles
applied, but it *still*
needs *your* content.

Adding content

Now comes the fun part (well, OK, *one* of the fun parts; all of this is fun, right?). Replace my `index.markdown` with your own—the one you made for your linear design. It must still be called `index.markdown`. Now run `dexy -r` again, and make sure you have a Dexy server running.

When you refresh the page in your browser, you'll see your narrow-width design.

Sectioning content

In order to lay things out on the screen (and yes, to denote content semantics), we're using the HTML `<section>` element to contain things, just like in the wireframe. Earlier I mentioned that you could copy each piece of content and paste it into its corresponding `<section>`. Since HTML is perfectly legal Markdown, a quick way to do this is to take the HTML that you already generated with Pandoc—everything between `<body>` and `</body>`—and paste it into `index.markdown`. That's not very elegant, though, because we don't get the advantages of Markdown.

Another way to do it is to use *hybrid* HTML/Markdown, where you use the `sections` from the wireframes in `index.markdown`, but you fill each with the corresponding Markdown text. This is hard to explain, so here's an example:

```
<section id="synopsis">
    In our industry, everything changes quickly, usually
for the better. We have more and better tools for creating
websites and applications that work across multiple
platforms. Oddly enough, design workflow hasn't changed
much, and what has changed is often for worse. Through
the years, increasing focus on bloated client deliverables
has hurt both content and design, often reducing these
disciplines to fill-in-the-blank and color-by-numbers
exercises, respectively. Old-school workflow is simply not
effective on our multiplatform web.
```

NOTE

`dexy serve` is simply Python's SimpleHTTPServer serving the contents of the `output-site` folder. But it sure is a lot easier to type.

```
Responsive Design Workflow explores:

    - A content-based approach to design workflow that's
grounded in our multi-platform reality, not fixed-width
Photoshop comps and overproduced wireframes
    - How to avoid being surprised by the realities of
multi-platform websites when practicing responsive web
design
    - How to better manage client expectations and
development requirements
    - A practical approach for designing in the browser
    - A method of design documentation that will prove more
useful than static Photoshop comps

</section>
```

We're using Markdown as usual, but surrounding certain content areas with the right `section` (or `div` if your prefer). This is flexible, since we don't need to change our templates, and it's still very human-readable and easy to edit, even for nontechnical people. Let's keep things as simple as possible and use this method here.

There *is* a third method, which the more technically inclined might prefer, and that is to separate the content of a page into chunks, and include these chunks in a template file. This requires more extensive knowledge of both Jinja and Dexy, but it offers consistency in your sectioning. If you look at `_base.html`, you can see how the includes are done. Here, you can see how the footer is included:

```
{% block footer -%}
    {% include 'macros/_footer.html' %}
{%- endblock %}
```

If you opted for this last method, you would add these types of includes for each section, and you do that in `_template.html`, or you could alternatively create several different templates for different types of pages. You would then need to use the `dexy.yaml` file to tell Dexy what to do with all those snippets.

While this method is useful for larger sites, we already have so many good things going for us solely by doing a web-based design; since our design is only a few mockup pages, let's simplify by doing our sectioning in Markdown files. Jinja templates are quite powerful, so feel free to research them more if you like!

In summary, to section your content, surround chunks of content in your Markdown file with the corresponding `section` elements from your wireframe, as in the example above. You'll end up with something like this:

```
<section id="book-title">
# Responsive Design Workflow

by Stephen Hay

</section>
<section id="synopsis">
    [ some content ]

</section>
<section id="purchase">
    [ some content ]

</section>
<section id="resources">
    [ some content ]

</section>
<section id="errata">
    [ some content ]

</section>
```

Your content will be between the `section` tags. Since only the sections are in HTML, this makes for a very readable file. Even nontechnical people will be able to edit it.

Keep in mind that Pandoc has to figure out what's HTML and what *needs to become* HTML, and that's not always simple, so Pandoc might get it wrong. My experience is that it's a good idea to leave a blank line before a closing HTML tag, as in the above example.

Note that we're using Pandoc, and if you choose to use another Markdown implementation, you'll have to go about things a bit differently to get the HTML/markdown combination working correctly. One thing I like about Pandoc is that it converts the things *between* normal HTML tags into HTML. Plain Markdown does not.

When you've finished sectioning your content, it's time to take a look at the configuration file.

Dexy's command center: The dexy.yaml file

When Dexy runs, it reads a configuration file. A few different formats are supported, from plain text to JSON. Arguably the most useful is YAML, which is human-readable yet structured.[5]

The `dexy.yaml` that I've included in the RDW template looks like this:

```
site:
    - .markdown|pandoc:
        - pandoc: { args: '-t html5' }

assets:
    - .css
    - .js
    - .png
    - .jpg
```

You can see that YAML consists of entries in the form:

```
Something:
    - sub-something
```

---

5 http://www.yaml.org

These are key/value pairs. In this configuration file we have two things: the pages of our site and the assets we'll use. Those are the main sections of the file. The assets section is a simple list of file types. Dexy will copy anything we list and do not pass through a filter. So, in this case, we're saying, "Copy all files with these extensions. These are our assets." It doesn't matter that the assets might be in different folders; Dexy will copy the enclosing folders over as well.

The `site` section is a little different, and it's a small sample of how powerful Dexy really is. Let's look at it again:

```
site:
    - .markdown|pandoc:
        - pandoc: { args: '-t html5' }
```

This says, "Our 'site' should be built from any pages with the `.markdown` extension. Find these pages and pass them through Pandoc. When you run Pandoc, run it with the argument `-t html5`."

If you've come to the conclusion that this does *the exact same thing* as running Pandoc straight from the command line, you are correct. In this simple example, that is indeed the case. But by Chapter 11, that will certainly *not* be the case. Plus, Dexy's "website reporter" is taking care of all the Jinja templating in our template files, adding things like navigation, the main content, and the footer. Thus, we're achieving more than simply using Pandoc at this point.

Use this simple default I've made for you, but play around a bit. If you use SVG images in your mockup, what should you do? Just add a line to your assets section:

```
assets:
    - .css
    - .js
    - .png
    - .jpg
    - .svg
```

Relatedly, if you're a hardcore nerd and want to hand-code all the HTML in your mockup, your configuration is simpler because you don't need a filter:

```
site:
    - .html
```

In this scenario, of course, you would have `index.html` instead of `index.markdown`.

We'll be doing a lot more with filters in Chapter 11 when we create a style guide.

Finishing your design mockup with CSS

At this point, we've fiddled around with a tool for long enough. You'll need to go through the steps we walked through in this chapter, adding to and changing your CSS so the page looks like your design at and between each breakpoint. The difference is that now you'll be doing this within Dexy as opposed to doing it in a static HTML file. Keep a Dexy server running, and you can update by running `dexy -r` and refreshing your page in your browser (**Figure 8.5**).

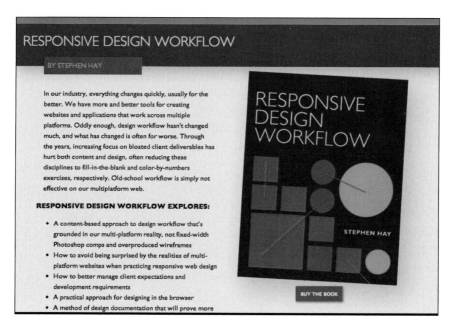

Figure 8.5
A finished design mockup. If you squint your eyes, it looks a bit like a Photoshop comp.

Remember that the hard part of design is the *thinking* part. It's coming up with the design in the first place. You've done that already. All you're doing now is creating a version of that design which is responsive and easily maintainable.

Multiple pages

Let's look at one more trick that Dexy and the RDW template offer you before we move on: you can (and often will) have a mockup that consists of several pages, and they'll be linked up automatically. When you looked at your page in the browser after Dexy was done with it, you should have noticed a single bullet point above the footer: "Home." This, believe it or not, is a menu with a single item—not very useful, in fact, unless you have more than one page in your mockup.

LEARNING CSS

If you're a visual designer without coding experience, don't sweat it! CSS is like chess: easy to learn but hard to master. Most of the CSS you'll need is in the easy-to-learn category. You might find CSS to be great fun, and it might inspire your future designs once you have some hands-on experience with it. CSS capabilities in browsers are getting better all the time, and there's some great stuff on the horizon.

CSS consists of several *modules*, each serving a specific purpose. Earlier in this book, we used the CSS Media Queries module to tell the browser when to apply specific CSS. There are modules for layout, fonts, backgrounds, borders, and even animations.

Personally, I think the best place to get an idea of what CSS is all about is at the W3C website: http://www.w3.org/Style/CSS/. That said, I think Mozilla's documentation about CSS is one of the absolute best resources available: https://developer.mozilla.org/en-US/docs/CSS.

CSS is a lot of fun, so just play around and experiment!

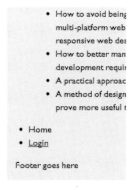

Figure 8.6
Dexy gives us a simple way to add navigation between pages.

The navigation is offered out of the box, and can be useful in many cases (**Figure 8.6**). Let's say you're doing a mockup of a home page, but also a mockup of a login page. The menu, which you can style as you please, allows you or your client to click back and forth between the pages. Then later, when you also mock up a registration form, the menu will pick it up automatically.

Let's try it. In your mockup directory (the folder that contains `dexy.yaml`) create a folder called `login.` Put a file in there called `index.markdown`, and add a heading, just so we can verify later that it is in fact the login page:

```
# This is the login page
```

Now run `dexy -r` again and visit the home page again in the browser. You should now see that the navigation includes a link to the login page, and the login page includes a link to the home page.

That's it—it's pretty simple. Of course, you're free to add a menu any way you please. You can hard-code them if you really, really want to. If you want to get rid of the default menu functionality for whatever reason, just remove the following line from the top of `_base.html`:

```
{% from 'macros/nav.jinja' import menu with context -%}
```

Jinja-geeks are also free to change the `nav.jinja` template to their heart's content.

What we've covered

In this chapter, you've learned how to combine your wireframes with your linear layout to form the foundation of a web-based mockup. You learned how to combine these two deliverables within the context of an SSG (static site generator). You've been introduced to Dexy and learned how to install it as well as how to pull in your existing assets. You learned what templates are and got a tiny glimpse into Dexy's configuration file and how filters work. And finally, you learned how to take advantage of Dexy's built-in optional site menu templates, making it child's play to add extra pages to your mockup and have Dexy generate a menu automatically.

Once you get your mockup done, it's time to present your design to your clients, your team, your stakeholders, and others. How you present web-based design mockups is every bit as important as the design itself. We'll talk about how to do this in the next chapter.

## 9

PRESENTATION, ROUND ONE: SCREENSHOT

"Rough layouts sell the idea better than polished ones."

—PAUL ARDEN

You (and perhaps your team) have been toiling away at your content inventory, your responsive content reference wireframes, your linear design, and your breakpoint graphs and you've designed for various breakpoints. You've visualized your design, the result of all these efforts, in the form of a web-based mockup.

Now you have to present your design to the client.

That is, you might. If you're not the one presenting the design to the client, someone else in your organization will. And you'll have to present it to him. I'll be frank: *if you're the designer,* unless you're the presentational equivalent of a wet towel, I'd recommend that *you* present your design to your clients.

For some, this is about 500 times worse than the command line. But it doesn't have to be, as I've learned. But before we get to that wisdom, there's an important point that will help make your presentation a success: what, exactly, are you going to present? Will you have the client click around in your prototype in a browser?

INVOLVE CLIENTS FROM THE BEGINNING

The decision to withhold your sketches and web-based mockup from the client team is the exception to the rule.

When working on every other step in the workflow, it's important to involve the client in the process. You can do a first draft of your content inventory *with* the client in the same room. When you've finished it, discuss it and make sure the client approves of it. You're not asking for approval as in, "I'm locking you in and you may never change it," but you *are* looking for a certain amount of commitment from the client that will allow you to move on to the next step, confident that you're on the right path.

Direct involvement also helps narrow the client's focus. Incremental, scope-limiting commitments from the client reduce the chances of requirements changing and help avoid the Big Reveal.

Repeat this process of involving the client at every step in your workflow. Involve the client when drafting what will become your deliverable, complete the deliverable, iterate if necessary, and get commitment. Each step brings you closer to an appropriate design and the boundaries of the work are very clear to everyone involved.

Designer Mark Boulton warns us to avoid what he calls The Big Reveal, the moment that you shock the hell out of your client with what you and your team have been working on for the past several weeks.[1] The Big Reveal is *bad*—very bad.

Avoiding the Big Reveal is easy: involve your client in every step of the workflow with one exception: *your sketches and the resulting web-based mockup* (for the time being.) This chapter explains why I recommend that, why you should present screenshots instead, and how to present those images.

Why not present in the browser right away?

I don't recommend involving your client in the web-based mockup step (or showing the sketches they're based on), and I don't suggest that you make your presentation at the end of these steps an interactive browser-based experience. Let's talk about why.

The presentation/realism balance

Presenting designs with an absence of detail involves a lot of risk. While avoiding detail in your design now and adding it later permits focus on feeling, atmosphere, and design language, this approach can come back to haunt you. Having not had an opportunity to ponder the details now, the client will eventually trip over them when they arrive. And this may have a huge impact on how the client feels about the design at that (later) point. If you first want to avoid detail, use mood boards to gauge how the client feels about abstractions like atmosphere: these are vague enough not to be confused with a complete design. They're not a design at all.

On the other hand, presenting realistic, detailed mockups *also* involves a lot of risk. Even if you avoid the Big Reveal, there's a period where you've worked in isolation to visualize the things you've been discussing and showing to

---

1 http://www.markboulton.co.uk/journal/responsive-summit-workflow

the client in the early steps. There's a point that the client is allowed to, and should, state her opinion and concerns. Call it the Small Reveal, if you like. But there is a reveal. And this is a point at which you'll either score a hole in one (it happens) or have to go back and iterate.

A web-based mockup is, or can be, just as detailed as a Photoshop file. So going web-based offers no advantage in terms of presentation or realism. The very advantage of web-based mockups, the fact that they're "designs in the browser," is also their biggest *disadvantage* when compared to static mockups: they introduce a whole new set of factors into the first presentation. I'm talking about interactive factors that don't come into play with static presentations, no matter how detailed. A planned Small Reveal can turn into a Big Reveal by revealing too much about the design at once.

NOTE
After you get feedback on your design, iteration is faster because CSS allows you to make changes quickly. You might not want to reveal just how quickly.

Static images are just that: images. You can tell this to your client and it will make sense to her. You can say, as I often have, "These are design impressions. They give an impression of how the site can look in some browsers. Be aware, though, that there's no *behavior*, no interaction. It's just about the impression; there's no *experience* that will come when you actually interact with the website in a browser."

This approach works well when presenting images. The client understands that she should *mainly* be concerned with discussion of *visual* aspects of design. You can make the client understand that it's not about content, although you present the content structure that's been determined. It's not about clicking or touching. It's not about the exact size of fonts on the screen.

It's about applied design language, communicating an identity, color, layout, *style* of imagery, and typography. It's about proportions, not pixels. The client can't interact with it, so there's no discussion about the speed of the hover transitions or that one-second flash of unstyled content while the page was loading.

If you present a web-based mockup—no matter what you say—these discussions *do* ensue, like it or not. When you present something with interactivity, the client is going to react to it. That's not the client's fault; it's human nature. It's the natural reaction of someone who sees something she's paying for.

So with all this talk of designing in the browser and now that you *have* a design in the browser, I'm advising you *not to present it in the browser*. At least, not yet.

Screenshots: Going from web-based (back) to images

You're thinking, "He told me to make a web-based design mockup, only to turn around and tell me to make screenshots of that mockup to present to the client?" Yes, I'm telling you that right now. But don't hate me yet.

Presenting images offers several advantages, in addition to those mentioned above:

◆ It de-emphasizes the malleability of the design. If something's in the browser, many clients know that little changes aren't all that hard to do. But you don't want to do little changes yet. You want commitment on the basic design.

◆ It avoids any problems, rendering or otherwise, which the client might encounter in the browser that could influence her opinion of the design. Present perception trumps plans for the future, so it doesn't matter if that font issue is on your bug tracker.

◆ It presents a format that's familiar to clients. They've seen Photoshop-created images for years, and still do.

◆ It doesn't give the impression that you're further along than you are. In Chapter 8, "Creating a Web-Based Design Mockup," we touched on the dangers of creating a design in the very medium for which we're designing: the client may question why the remaining work will cost so much time and money since the work is already "so far along."

Personally, I find these reasons compelling enough to present images *the first time* I show a design to a client. The focus is mostly on the visual design and not on any implementation factors.

What we're doing here is using the implicit psychology at work in design presentations to our advantage. We're avoiding counterproductive discussions about things that don't matter just yet, and we're creating another opportunity to get even more client commitment. Client commitments hold the rope on your project. When you're this far up the mountain, they keep you from falling too far down.

After getting client commitment on the direction set forth in the images, a logical next step is to show web-based mockups. At this point it's not overwhelming or distracting to deal with issues raised by interactivity because you have a commitment on the design direction. Then you can produce relatively quick iterations on the mockups until there's enough commitment to begin site production.

When you already have a web-based mockup, how do you get static images? You take screenshots. Not special screenshots—just normal, everyday, run-of-the mill screenshots. However, since you have a responsive mockup, you'll take advantage of that fact by taking screenshots of your designs *at varying viewport widths* (**Figure 9.1**). That's the difference. Say goodbye to multiple Photoshop files that have to be edited individually with every design change.

WE'RE NOT "TRICKING" CLIENTS

This isn't about misleading clients into thinking we're working in Photoshop and will go and create a prototype upon approval (although I've often joked about that). It's about using the right tools at the right moment in the process in order to have the most positive effect on the project as a whole. In fact, I recommend that you *not* mention that you already have a web mockup. You don't mention every application you use to create other deliverables, so there's no need to start now. As far as your client is concerned, the browser is simply the Photoshop that *you* used to create the images you're presenting. How you'll use that mockup next is irrelevant at this moment.

That said, if asked, *never* lie to your client. A good relationship can never be built on lies. Bend the truth a bit, but only if you can do it right: "Yes, we support the practice of designing in the browser and I do have a web-based mockup of the design I'm presenting to you today. Because it's just a mockup at this point and not thoroughly tested in most browsers, we want to avoid any unexpected issues that might distract from the real purpose of this session, which is to come to an agreement on the direction of the visual design. Once we've done that, we'll definitely finish testing the mockup so you can experience how this design will work on various browsers and platforms."

That's a fair, albeit wordy, response and it's quite true, although testing of the mockup *might* not be as extensive as implied.

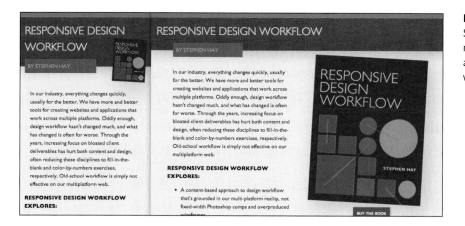

Figure 9.1
Screenshots of mockups can be taken at various viewport widths.

How to make screenshots

I must be kidding, right? Well, maybe a little. You know how to make screenshots, and you can create them any way you like. There are, however, two ways of creating them:

◆ Manual

◆ Automated

The method you choose will depend on your personal preferences, your willingness to tinker (or lack thereof), and the number of screenshots and iterations you expect to make.

Manual screenshots

Making screenshots manually is easy. In the worst-case scenario, you simply press "print screen" or use your system's built-in screen-capture utility. The more options a screen-capture utility has, the better: I recommend showing no browser chrome in your screenshots, to keep them browser-agnostic, if you will (**Figure 9.2**). It's not the browser that's important here, and your client probably knows you're designing a website, anyway. Cropping menus and chrome out of screenshots is tedious work, so your choice of tool can help avoid that.

NOTE
Many firms add browser chrome around their images to make them look like they're in a browser. I've avoided this for years, and had my former teams do the same. We're removing any reference to how the design might look in specific browsers, and chrome doesn't make your design look better.

Since this is all about responsive design, I recommend taking a screenshot of each of your designed screens, at each major breakpoint. You know what these are by this phase. Since this is about creating design impressions, different platforms and browsers are not an issue yet, not for this specific deliverable. You can simply open your preferred browser (provided that your design looks as intended) and resize the window until its width matches your first breakpoint. Take a screenshot. Adjust the window to the next breakpoint. Take a screenshot. Continue until you've got a screenshot at each major breakpoint. Do this for each of the screens you designed.

Taking screenshots manually is easy. It's actually kind of fun, at least until you have to tweak something in your mockup and make new ones. That's where automated screenshots come in handy.

Automated screenshots

Thanks to *scriptable browsers,* it's possible to write scripts to automate the taking of screenshots. One of these browsers is called PhantomJS, which is a *headless* WebKit browser that lets you control it via JavaScript. *Headless* basically means that there's no graphical user interface; you can't actually *see*

Figure 9.2
Including browser chrome on a design, though a common practice, serves little purpose and doesn't improve the perception of the design.

Figure 9.3
With PhantomJS, you can't see the browser, but it's there.

the browser. And since it's a WebKit browser, it's similar to (though *not* the same as) Apple's Safari and Google's Chrome browsers. PhantomJS is often used to automate the testing of websites, but it also provides the ability to take screenshots (**Figure 9.3**).

As with Dexy, this will take some setting up and familiarization. But once you've done that, you'll find it simple to add new screenshots. Another benefit of the automated approach is that we'll be doing automated screenshots when creating design documentation in Chapter 11, "Creating Design Guidelines." Any experience you gain now will make things that much easier later on.

INSTALL PHANTOMJS

A utility called CasperJS makes scripting for PhantomJS that much easier. If you want to follow along, you'll need to download both PhantomJS and CasperJS. Go to each of the websites,[2] download the packages, and follow the installation instructions. It's really as simple as that. Now you can test whether you have them by running this in your terminal:

```
$ phantomjs --version
```

Remember that you don't have to type the dollar sign. That's your prompt. That command should return a version number. At the time of this writing, mine is 1.7.0. If you've got PhantomJS, follow that with the test for CasperJS:

```
$ casperjs --version
```

This should also give you a version number. If you have a version number for both, that means Phantom and Casper are installed and you're good to go.

2 http://phantomjs.org and http://casperjs.org

WRITING YOUR SCREENSHOT SCRIPT

We're going to do all of our scripting with CasperJS, because it makes things relatively easy compared to scripting PhantomJS directly. To start, create a file called `screenshots.js` in your mockup's directory and type out the following lines:

```
var casper = require('casper').create();
```

Save the file. Create a folder called `screenshots` in your mockup folder as well. Now, run `dexy serve` and note the URL that Dexy gives you. For me, that's `http://localhost:8085`. You'll want to use the URL Dexy gives you in your script. Start off by typing the following:

```
casper.start();

var baseUrl = "http://localhost:8085"; // The URL should be
  →the URL you got from "dexy serve"
```

This tells CasperJS to start and sets the base URL. Now let's create an *array* of viewport widths at which we'd like to take screenshots (to non-coders: array means "list" but sounds more impressive):

```
var breakpoints = [400, 600, 900, 1200];
```

Once we're on a page, we want to take screenshots of it at each viewport width. The most efficient way to do this is by looping through the various widths:

```
casper.open(baseUrl).then(function() {
    breakpoints.forEach(function(breakpoint) {
        casper.viewport(breakpoint, 800).
          →capture('screenshots/' + breakpoint + '.png', {
            top: 0,
            left: 0,
            width: breakpoint,
            height: casper.evaluate(function(){ return
              →document.body.scrollHeight; })
        });
    });
});
```

This reads almost like English: "Open the base URL. Then, for each of the breakpoints in our breakpoint list, set the viewport to that width and a height of (at least) 800px. Take a screenshot of the page and save the resulting file as '[breakpoint].png' in the screenshots folder."

By looping in this way, we make it easy to add and remove breakpoints, simply by adding or removing a value to or from the *breakpoints* array.

The last line of the file should be:

```
casper.run();
```

Save the file and run this script by running:

```
$ casperjs screenshots.js
```

After a few seconds, the prompt will reappear. Run the `ls` command in the command line or otherwise look in the screenshots folder. You should see a collection of PNG files with the breakpoints as file names. Open these and check them out. You just automated your screenshots! Now, when you make changes to your mockup, all you have to do is run `casperjs screenshots.js` in your terminal, wait a bit, and you've got your screenshots!

What if your mockup is more than one page? In that case, you'll have to loop twice: once through a list of pages, and once through the breakpoints for each page. First, add a list of pages and the name of the screenshot folder:

```
var baseUrl = 'http://localhost:8085';
var breakpoints = [400, 600, 900, 1200];
var links = [
    '', // an empty string means the home page
    '/chapter1/' // if you have more levels it would be
    →something like /chapter1/errata/
];
var screenshotFolder = 'screenshots';
```

Since `links` and `screenshotFolder` are *strings* (text instead of numbers), they need to be in quotes as shown. Next, create a function to construct the name of the file. This allows for simple entry of links into the array and replaces the slashes in the links with underscores in the filenames.

> **NOTE**
>
> JavaScripters should be aware that we're using `var` on each line for readability, as opposed to combining them with commas.

```
function nameFile(link, breakpoint) {
    if (link == '') {
        var name = 'home';
    } else {
        var name = link;
    }
    return screenshotFolder + '/' + name.replace(/\//g,'_')
    ⇥+ breakpoint + '.png';
}
```

Finally, rewrite the screen-capturing function so it opens the pages one by one and then captures the screen at each viewport width. Replace the current capture function with this one:

```
links.forEach(function(link) {
    casper.thenOpen(baseUrl + link, function () {
        breakpoints.forEach(function(breakpoint) {
            casper.viewport(breakpoint, 800).
            ⇥capture(nameFile(link, breakpoint), {
            top: 0,
            left: 0,
            width: breakpoint,
            height: casper.evaluate(function(){ return
            ⇥document.body.scrollHeight; })
            });
        });
    });
});
```

NOTE

JavaScripters should be aware that, at the time of this writing, it was necessary to trigger a synchronous reflow in WebKit, ensuring that the contents of the window adapt to the new window size. This is the reason for reading the scrollHeight.

Depending on how many pages and viewports you have, this is a pretty "expensive" script and will take several seconds to run. Remember, it's taking screenshots for you; it's still much faster than doing them manually. By the way, you can use this script to capture pages from *any* web page at various resolutions. Just plug in the desired base URL and pages, save, and run it again.

When you're finished, you should have a collection of PNG images in your screenshots folder, all perfect and ready to show to your client. And I know you can't wait for your client to make changes so you can implement them in your mockup and run `casperjs screenshots.js` again. This is all kinds of fun!

Presenting screenshots

Once you have your screenshots, there are three common ways of presenting them:

1. Print them out and paste them on presentation board (this is *really* old school, although you can print them *in addition to* using a projector).

2. Show them on your laptop screen while your client and stakeholders huddle around and strain their lower backs.

3. Use a projector.

I prefer number three. Projecting makes viewing easy for everyone, provided you consider things like lighting and use a good-quality projector. You control the pace of what is seen. Presenting on board can work, but it can also give the impression that you're only painting pretty pictures. Everything you do successfully with a piece of technology in the presence of your client will either add or subtract from the perception of your competence. Show the client that you control the tech and use it to your advantage.

Another advantage of on-screen or projector presentations is that you can switch out of your presentation to other examples or resources, and then switch right back.

Unless you're presenting to only one or two people, avoid laptop-screen presentations. There are viewing-angle issues, and sometimes it involves people moving into each other's personal space. Again, the more comfortable everyone is, the better.

Lastly, paste your screenshots into presentation software and run through them that way (**Figure 9.4**). Heck, you can even add a title slide and some important points in between. Use a handheld presentation clicker (bonus points if it has a laser pointer). Few things are worse for a client than watching someone fumble around opening screenshot number 27 by hand, shuffling windows around via a trackpad.

NOTE

Since PDFs can be presented in full-screen mode in most PDF readers, there's virtually no limit to which software you use to create your presentations, so long as you can export as a PDF. Adobe InDesign and other page layout applications are great for this.

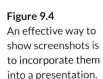

Figure 9.4
An effective way to show screenshots is to incorporate them into a presentation.

Keep the discussions of screenshots on the visual part of the design. The object is first to discover if you're on the right visual track. If you're not, any other design discussion is pointless. If it turns out that you *are* on track, that's a good moment to open up the discussion to other things that the client might have noticed, such as specific issues related to content.

You'll only have to present screenshots again if your client really dislikes your design and you have to go back to the drawing board. Honestly, this should be *extremely* rare if your client has accompanied you through the workflow thus far. There can't be much that unpleasantly surprises her at this point. Still, it can happen. It's possible that the client just doesn't like what you've done. If that's the case, use screenshots again when you've adjusted the design. Otherwise, if the client is on your side, you'll be presenting in browsers from now on.

We'll still be using screenshots for design documentation. But for now, let's look at the final iterative phase before your design can go into production.

## 10

PRESENTATION, ROUND TWO: IN THE BROWSER

*Instead of waiting for perfection,
run with what you've got,
and fix it as you go.*

—PAUL ARDEN

After that last chapter about screenshots, I'm sure you want to get back to the browser so badly that you're having withdrawal symptoms. Remain calm; we're headed straight back into the browser—in fact, not one, not two, but several browsers on every device you have!

Once your client approves of the general direction you're taking the design, there's no longer a need to present images. At this point, more detailed feedback is necessary on all page types, as opposed to the few that you presented as screenshots. Since you have a web-based mockup, now is the time to show all the stakeholders how your design works in the browser. *Any* browser.

This iterative process isn't only good for your client. You're the designer, so you know how you want things to look and work. This is your opportunity to see if things work as planned, or if you need to make some adjustments or explain and create documentation. Factors you didn't know about will come to light and influence your design. New details your client mentions will add challenges. More or new information about content can mean you need to change direction when you discover that the list of 10 headlines should actually be 100 items that need a filtering mechanism.

Once you start looking at your design in a variety of devices and on a variety of platforms, you'll discover that it doesn't look as it should; you'll find many bugs. I repeat: you'll find many bugs in your design.

You'll find many bugs in your design

Obviously you checked your design in a browser; if you followed the steps in the last chapter, then your screenshots were made in a WebKit browser. But there are many other browsers, for desktops/laptops, tablets, smartphones, feature phones, televisions, game consoles, whatever. Your site will look like crap in at least one, and probably several, of these environments. This is sobering (which is a *good* thing), but there's no cause for worry. If you're the project developer, you have a choice ahead:

1. Fix the bugs in your design.
2. Leave the bugs and document the way it's *supposed* to be.

The choice you make depends on several factors:

◆ Are you a developer? Do you have enough experience to solve the issues on your own or with a little help from a coworker?

◆ Does your site need to look *perfect* in *every* situation? Probably not, but it should not look broken, and it should absolutely be usable in any but the most uncommon environment.

◆ Which will take more time: fixing the design in your mockup or documenting how it should look and work in a given browsing environment?

◆ Are there errors in your code or simply limitations or bugs in the browsing environment?

◆ How much time and money have you budgeted?

Consider each of these factors before deciding what to do. In the next chapter, we'll talk about how to create design documentation. Nevertheless, I would advise you to try to fix any design issues *in your web-based mockup*, the above factors permitting. Documenting specific scenarios that aren't represented accurately in the mockup can quickly become time-consuming. You'll need to *visualize* how a given screen or component *should* look or behave in a given context. If you have to do this for every little situation that pops up, your world is going to become really unhappy in a big hurry.

Collaboration and communication

Two traps can put up heavy-duty roadblocks to project completion: thinking "We'll tackle that during development" and "Hey Tim, look: on this tablet the menu bar wraps to a new line. Remember to fix that." Well, OK, those sound like the same trap.

The responsive design workflow can help you avoid traps like this one, largely because anyone can be brought in at every single phase. At every point there's a useful deliverable that's designed to either communicate choices, problems, and requirements, or document existing ones.

Take advantage of these deliverables. Building in communication during each phase avoids the syndrome often seen in web workplaces today of using the *assembly line approach*: Maker A hands off Deliverable A to Maker B, who hands off Deliverable B to Maker C, and so forth. This traditional approach shovels all the manure, including increased deadline pressure, straight into the lap of the last person on the assembly line. Often, those people are the developers.

That's not fair, and can be easily avoided by *communicating* and *working together*. Crazy, eh?

The workflow presented in this book facilitates the creation of design deliverables that each involve input from several disciplines. They *all* involve designers to some degree, and developers can also be involved early. Content inventories are not only used to create wireframes, but also are absolutely essential throughout the project. This process radically decreases the chance that designers and developers will get saddled with a bunch of segmented deliverables at the last minute, with a monstrous deadline approaching.

Presenting screenshots allowed us to focus discussion on visual design, and now presenting web-based design mockups in the browser lets us collaborate on practically all aspects of the design on the front end. Potential pitfalls will be spotted by coworkers who are viewing it through the filter of their disciplines—things that might not have been noticed when looking at Photoshop files or screenshots. Developers can easily see how certain components should work, and begin devising an appropriate development approach.

Perhaps most importantly, discussions about "the website not looking like the design" should be virtually eliminated, since the design itself is in the very medium for which it was designed. Want to avoid discussions about the way a site *might* look in browser X? Show the design in browser X. You can even show the design as it appears in *multiple browsers*. You will effectively eliminate visual surprises. You need expect only that the developers will follow the design instructions closely and use the mockup as a guide.

How to present your interactive mockups

At the screenshot presentation stage, you should have begun warming your client up to the fact that, upon agreement regarding the design direction, you would be presenting in the browser from that point on. Until this approach becomes the norm, you can list the advantages I've mentioned repeatedly throughout the book to your client. You can present it as an added value, because it *is* in fact an added value, to you and to your client.

As with your screenshot presentation, a projector is very important for your main presentation. This time you'll be projecting your web-based mockup "live" in the same way you would a beta site. However, walk through the design slowly, taking the time to answer any questions, just as you would if you were presenting static comps.

Use devices to impress

Many designers come up with really interesting ideas that can be only partially expressed in a visual manner. This is mainly because, as I've mentioned before, web design is not only visual. It's a combination of visual elements, content, and interaction; it's an *experience*. (That's why we have user experience designers, but that's another term for another discussion some other time.) Think of it this way: everyone working on the website is contributing to the user experience, and presenting your web-based mockup in browsers and on real devices is a fantastic way to introduce your client to that experience.

Take some different devices with you to a presentation. At my company, before there were smartphones, we tested our websites on feature phone browsers. Very few people visited sites on their phones, but that was no less impressive for clients when I whipped out my Sony Ericsson K800i and showed them that their website worked, *even on a phone.*

Nowadays, clients increasingly expect their sites to work on multiple devices. They don't always expect to see their *designs* working in those devices in the design phase. Wow them. Show the design on various devices.

This is quite easy to do if you take a laptop computer with you to the presentation: make sure all devices are on the same local network and serve the web mockup from your laptop. (If you don't have access to a network, see if you can turn your own laptop into an access point.) You can simply browse through the mocked-up pages, and invite the members of the client team to do the same, even on *their own* devices.

Explaining your design

Since your client has already seen the visual design in screenshot form, now is the time to emphasize the tangible aspects of the design in the browser. There's no harm in explaining less obvious design aspects of various breakpoints: the type growing or shrinking, when smaller or larger images are switched in, how you determined device classes. These subtleties, when presented correctly, can make the client even happier with what you've done. (In my experience, these are things the clients themselves love to point out to others; in a sense, you're enabling them to show off.)

This is the time to show the client how the design *responds* to changes in orientation, pixel density, and any other factors or device features that trigger changes. The first time you walk through the mockups, it's a good idea to be your client's guide, rather than having her go through them herself straight away. This is so you control what is seen, where the focus is directed. Once you've walked through a few important screens, invite your client to browse through them herself to get a feel for how it works. The initial walkthrough with you anticipates some questions she might have, and helps to create a more positive experience ("Oh, I love it how we get that extra column when we change to landscape orientation").

Your words and phrasing are important when framing the principle of content-first responsive design for the client. Start out by focusing on how the base content and functionality is accessible on less-capable and smaller devices. Then build gradually, revealing the extra features you get as device capabilities increase. This can profoundly change the way people think about responsive design. "When I see it on a phone, all the content gets stacked vertically" becomes "We start with the content stacked vertically; now look at what happens on this tablet." This is a powerful concept, a distinction that my own clients really appreciate knowing about.

Testing and client review

An advantage of web-based design mockups is the potential for testing at this relatively early stage. Usability, accessibility, and A/B testing are all possible with many web-based mockups. It's certainly worth considering, as change costs are lower in this phase than during or after production, when testing is usually performed. There are fewer factors at this stage, so if something is found, it's easier to isolate the cause and fix it. Test the design first and do the same test again after production. Adjusting your design in response to

DON'T BE *TOO* REALISTIC

When reviewing something so tangible and realistic in actual browsers on actual devices, the client may forget that she's looking at a design as opposed to a finished website. It's important to emphasize that this is in fact the case. I find three things helpful in this regard:

1. Keep mentioning it. Listen carefully to the client's comments (which is a good practice anyway) and respond to any comment that might be related to a browser bug with something like, "Please remember that this is only the design and not the final implementation." Of course, don't repeat that same line over and over, unless you want to get rid of your client quickly.

2. Explain design features, not functions. Not getting into discussions about how forms will be processed on the server, how content managers will input their content, and similar subjects will emphasize that this isn't the finished product, despite the realism of the visuals. Sometimes, when I'm presenting a design, the client sees a form element and the discussion quickly detours into something like server-side caching or which email newsletter software she wants to use. Those are fun subjects for some, but not for me, and not right now. Of course, questions and discussion about things like hover effects and similar client-side, front-end subjects are all fair game.

3. Use a table of contents. Don't try to make an actual prototype site. In other words, even if your designed pages follow one another in a natural flow, consider not linking them directly, but rather getting from one page to another via a table of contents that contains links to all of the designed pages. This removes any kind of navigation flow, which reinforces the knowledge that this is still design.

testing means that you'll usually find fewer issues in production. If clients balk at the expense of this "extra" testing, try to make the case that it will be a savings in end.

Client review

Of course, the most obvious form of testing in this phase is walking the client through the mockups and watching her reaction. We don't think of this as testing, but you'll need to respond in some way to every single comment your client makes: act on it, discuss it, or dismiss it.

As a general rule, never dismiss a client comment out of hand. It's in poor taste and gives the impression you're not listening and that you don't take your client's opinion seriously. At the end of the day, you're a designer serving the client's goals, not an artist. This person is paying you. At least consider your client's concerns (or pause and look upward at an angle and scratch your chin and *look* like you're considering) and then respond with reasoned points to support your position without being argumentative.

Since design sometimes feels more akin to prostitution than to art ("Sure, I can do that for you, but it will cost you more"), some clients will pretty much expect you to execute whatever they want. This is frustrating. Few things are worse than a client saying, "Please make all the text magenta," when you *know* it's going to look *awful* (and hard to read!). You might think of opening up your developer tools and changing the color on the fly to show them how stupid that idea really is. I don't recommend it because there's always the risk that she'll say, "Yes! It's beautiful!" and it's not good practice in general. Try to uncover the client's concern or the problem she's trying to solve.

Most often, I find that the element of time helps these discussions. Make the client wait at least a little while to see changes—this will give you time to think about them and perhaps come up with a solution that keeps your design as intended *and* solves the problem. And you could then still decide to show them how terrible magenta body text looks; it's a one-line change in CSS.

In order to approach iterations in a sane manner, it's best to take good notes.

NOTE

Linking designed pages can be useful under certain circumstances, such as for usability testing on the design.

NOTE

Remember when I say client, I mean anyone who must approve your work in order for the project to continue. This can be the actual client as well as other stakeholders or managers involved in the decision process.

Take good notes

Taking notes is important, as I'm sure you've experienced in your own work. It creates a record of requests, which makes it easier to identify new requests that extend outside the project scope. Also, notes provide a to-do list for designers and developers during the revision process. After all, you want to avoid discussions starting with, "I mentioned to you on the phone that I'd like the logo bigger." "No, I don't recall…" "Well, then maybe you should pay more attention." Ouch.

At the beginning of a design review session in which you walk through your mockups, inform your client that you'll be making note of requests made regarding the design. If you don't take the notes yourself, someone on your team can do this for you. It's important to announce the note taking before-hand, because this subtly lets the client know that after-the-fact requests under the guise of "don't you remember I said that…" will not be possible. And let's be honest: we all forget plenty of things we don't write down. Take notes.

How you take these notes is up to you: paper, text document, mind map—all of them work just fine. However, this is another case where developer inge-nuity can help us, by allowing us to make notes *on the mockups in the browser*.

NOTE TAKING ON YOUR MOCKUPS (IN THE BROWSER)

There are several apps that allow you to create *sticky notes* on your design. I thought it might be nice to do something similar, but wanted to rely on simple code that I could use in my mockups themselves, without having to rely on a third-party app (though there's nothing inherently wrong with that). I had played around a bit with **localStorage**, having used it to create a simple responsive web app. localStorage is easy to use; I learned about it mostly from write-ups and examples by Remy Sharp[1] and Christian Heilmann.[2]

Wouldn't localStorage be a way to type notes onto a page and save them? Sure it would, and it is, in fact, used by some of the web page *sticky note* apps out there. In the interest of keeping things relatively simple but extendable

localStorage, once referred to as HTML5 localStorage but now part of W3C's Web Storage API, provides a storage object for you in the browser. It's considered similar to cookies, but offers a lot more space (5 MB). See the specification for more details.

---

1 http://html5demos.com/contenteditable

2 http://24ways.org/2010/html5-local-storage/ This article is older, but still very useful for understanding what localStorage is and how it works.

for those who want to do more, I cooked up my own little note-taking functionality, inspired by Sharp's demo (**Figure 10.1**).

If you look at **Figure 10.2** and squint your eyes, it kind of looks like a sticky note. Well, OK, you have to squint *really hard*. Seriously, though, the intention isn't to look like a sticky note, but to have a place available on each mockup to record notes on the fly.

Figure 10.1
Remy Sharp's `contenteditable` demo shows how `contenteditable` can be used in conjunction with localStorage.

Figure 10.2
Our note-taking functionality kind of looks like a sticky note, doesn't it? Maybe just a little?

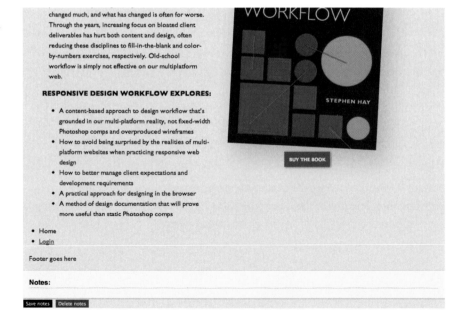

Thanks to localStorage, you can save these notes in the browser. They'll only be available on the computer that was used to enter them, though. If you're in the habit of creating a complete record of all notes for yourself or your clients, you can copy and paste each note into one large text document for recordkeeping purposes, but I find it useful to leave the notes on the mockups as well.

Let's take a look at how to create this easy-to-implement but handy functionality before mentioning a couple of its uses.

NOTE-TAKING "APP"

You don't have to learn how to use localStorage if you simply want to take advantage of this note-taking functionality. Just read through the examples by Sharp and Heilmann, who know more about it and can explain things much better than I can here, and you should be able to understand the code that follows below.

This is JavaScript, and we want the code to be on every page of our mockup, just before the `</body>` tag at the end of the HTML file. If you're using Dexy to generate your mockups, then you need only put the following code at that point in the `_base.html` file in your project folder:

```
<script>
    var title = document.title;
    var note = document.querySelector('#notes');
    var saveButton = document.querySelector('#save-notes');
    var clearButton = document.querySelector('#clear-notes');

    function getNote() {
        if (localStorage['note_'+title]) {
            note.innerHTML = localStorage['note_'+title];
        }
    }

    function saveNote() {
        localStorage['note_'+title] = note.innerHTML;
    }
```

NOTE

While I recommend localStorage here as a way to quickly take notes on a mockup page, don't rely on it on for permanent storage of your notes. Browsers, especially during updates and crashes, might delete your content. Always copy notes to a more permanent file for safekeeping.

```
function deleteNote() {
    if (localStorage['note_'+title]) {
        note.innerHTML = '';
        delete localStorage['note_'+title];
    }
}

document.addEventListener('DOMContentLoaded', getNote);

savebutton.addEventListener('click', function(e) {
    saveNote();
});

clearbutton.addEventListener('click', function(e) {
    deleteNote();
});
</script>
```

Without going into the exact details of how localStorage works, here's the gist of this code in plain language:

"First, define what the title is (it should be a unique title per page, otherwise you'll simply keep overwriting the same storage space) and what the notes area is, as well as the buttons we'll use for saving and deleting notes. Then, tell the browser how to get notes, how to save them, how to delete them, and make sure that when I call up the page, the saved note gets called up on the page as well. Lastly, attach the save and delete functions to their respective buttons on the page."

This is *really* simple, yet it works like a charm. But wait, we have no buttons in our mockups yet, and no area to actually type in our notes. Let's add those. Place the following right above the `<script>` tag:

```
<div id="notes" contenteditable></div>
<button id="save-notes">Save notes</button>
<button id="clear-notes">Delete notes</button>
```

It should be obvious what the two buttons are. The div is where we'll actually be typing in the notes. You can style both the buttons and the div as you please.

Normally, you can't just start typing into a div. So we're setting `contenteditable` here, so we *can*. This isn't supported in all browsers, however, so you're restricting yourself here to using a browser that supports it. That's a good thing, actually, because you'll be using a fairly modern and standards-compliant browser to display your mockups, which is a good idea.

While you can style these note-taking elements however you like, I've created a simple default for you that creates a result similar to the one pictured in Figure 10.2. Just add the following CSS to the bottom of the `base.css` file for your mockup:

```css
/* Notes */
#notes {
    min-height: 2em;
    background-color: lightyellow;
    color: gray;
    padding: 1em;
    font: medium/1.5 sans-serif;
    box-shadow: 1px 1px 5px silver;
}
#notes::before {
    content: 'Notes:';
    display: block;
    color: black;
    font-weight: bold;
    border-bottom: 1px dotted tan;
}
#clear-notes,
#save-notes {
    border: none;
    background-color: black;
    color: gainsboro;
}
#clear-notes,
#save-notes:hover {
    background-color: dimgray;
    cursor: pointer;
}
```

Tweak these to your heart's desire. In fact, if you're comfortable with JavaScript, there's an amazing array of things you can do with this simple little app: have the note-taking area appear at the touch of a specific key so it's not always in view, have it slide in from the top or side of the screen, make it look like a real sticky note, even animate it with CSS! Personally, I like the simple approach. But part of the fun of web technology is discovery and experimentation, so have some fun with it.

Using your notes and making revisions

The short pieces of code above combine to give you a note-taking functionality at the bottom of each page of the mockup. Each person browsing on a device will see and in many cases be able to use the note-taking app, but each browser's notes are saved only *within that specific browser*. Thus, your client will not see your notes and you cannot see hers. There are ways to do that, but they go way beyond the scope of this book.

I recommend *showing* your design mockups on many devices and in many browsers, but taking notes in a solid, new browser on a laptop computer. This isn't absolutely necessary, but for me, my laptop is my main working machine while my other devices are primarily for testing and demonstration purposes. This means that when I get to work adjusting a design, I have the notes right there.

Simply type requests and other comments in the notes field on the page being discussed. The client will no doubt understand that the notes are not a part of the design, but it doesn't hurt to mention it. Continue this process until all of the mockups have been discussed.

When you're ready to revise, simply call up the mockup you want to work on and look at your notes. Then make the appropriate design changes and move on to the next one. When you've finished doing changes to a mockup, you can decide whether to keep your notes so that you have a note history per mockup, or you can opt to delete them (there's a button for that).

When showing your revised mockups, you can scroll down to the notes and reiterate what was requested the last time, and then show how you tackled the problem (**Figure 10.3**).

NOTE

Remember that localStorage has a 5 MB limit per domain (and your local server is one domain). Also be aware that notes are stored per domain (so notes taken on 127.0.0.1:8000 will not be available on example.com) and that they're kept in browser storage. For these reasons, it's a good idea to copy all notes to a text file. If you're a hardcore developer, perhaps you can write a script to do that for you.

Notes:
- Colors in header don't match colors on book cover
- Navigation isn't styled correctly
- What do we want in the footer? Does there even need to be a footer?
- Book cover is too dominant
- Please make the logo bigger ;-)

Save notes Delete notes

Figure 10.3
Notes can be used in subsequent client meetings to review past requests.

VERSION CONTROL FOR REVISIONS

Developers have the advantage of being able to have a problem, think of a solution, *and build that solution*. A lot of advice in this book is about taking advantage of tools outside of the designer's realm (mainly from the developer's realm) to improve your workflow. This is certainly the case when it comes to version control systems.

Developers use version control to track changes to source code. They write code and commit it to a version control repository. It's automatically marked with a version number. When changes are made, these changes are committed and marked with their own new version number. Using a system like this means two important things for designers:

1. You can always work in the newest version without being confronted with the clutter of multiple files with version numbers in the file names, or other such workarounds.

2. If you mess up, or for some reason your client says, "Let's go with the previous version," you can *roll back* to the version in question.

Version control systems, such as git or svn, can be *very* complex. I use git and *most* of the time I need only a few simple commands. Something really has to go wrong before I need to do anything more complicated. Also, there's so much easy-to-understand material available about git on the web that I've never run into any problems I can't solve.

Since most of your deliverables in this workflow are text-based (including your designs, which are actually in code), I recommend that you look into using version control for all your deliverables. This way, all your changes to content inventories, wireframes, breakpoint graphs, mockups, and everything else will remain intact. Once you start using version control, you'll never want to work without it.

http://git-scm.com/book is a popular git reference, but a simple Google search on git or version control will quickly land you on a good resource. And don't forget to ask your developer friends; in my experience, the best developers love to share information!

This process is the same as the traditional design revision process: rinse and repeat until all necessary parties are satisfied that the project can move on to production.

If you're at that point, hooray! You've almost made it to the end of this process. The client has approved your designs and given the go-ahead to move on to production, where developers will implement your design (or you'll implement your own design). Most designers stop at this point, but for yourself, the developer(s), and your clients, it can be extremely useful to document some or all aspects of the design in a human-readable form. Design documentation, sometimes called a *style guide*, can be helpful in this regard. We'll discuss how to create this in the next chapter.

CREATING DESIGN GUIDELINES

"As much as I love things in flux, I love them within a frame of reference—a consistent reassurance that at least and at last I am the one responsible for every detail."

—MASSIMO VIGNELLI

One day in college my graphic design professor brought in a set of design guidelines from Apple Computer. We'd been working on logos and identity design, and here was this book (it was literally a book) with rules regarding the Apple style and how to use it. This was back when Apple had the multicolored logo, an apple with a rainbow in it—at least, that's the way it appeared to me. I was struck by how complete it seemed. It described an entire design system. This was light years ahead of what we were doing in class: spending weeks and weeks to come up with a logo and create some simple stationery with it. This was the real work.

After studying that manual for days—how type was used, how ads were created—I started thinking about the manual itself. What a crazy amount of work it must have been to write the book, design it, and create it. All the design decisions had been painstakingly recorded so that other designers, anyone implementing Apple's design system, could do so in a way that was consistent with everything else that had been done. The book solidified all of that creativity into a set of rules, a recipe of sorts. It was amazing to me.

Years later, I found myself creating similar guidelines, though admittedly on a smaller scale than the Apple manual. I didn't much like doing that work. The creative part was finished, I had designed the building blocks for identity systems, and documenting them wasn't my favorite activity. In fact, on most projects, I didn't have to. So when it wasn't requested of me, I didn't document. When I had to account for additional parts of the system, say, when we were asked to create an annual report, I would simply look at all the other stuff I had done for the same client and try to extract the system out of that. Let me tell you, that takes a lot of time.

Had I taken the time to document the system, I would have had a set of building blocks that I could pull out and use as a basis for my design. The saying "good judgment comes from experience, and experience comes from bad judgment," which has been attributed to just about everybody, applies here. I began documenting the systems I designed, even if only for my own use in future projects for the same client.

Design manuals and the web

Design guidelines, style manuals, design standards, identity guidelines—they all mean basically the same thing, and they've been created for print design for many years. However, for websites, they're a bit less commonplace. That's changing at the time of this writing; articles like the one that Anna Debenham wrote for 24ways.org have sparked interest in the subject within the web design industry.[1]

Documenting design systems for websites is at least as important as for print. Since websites aren't always designed by the same people who design print collateral, we can't always expect that a traditional design standards manual will include all the necessary information about the web design. Of course, it will depend on the client, the design firm, and the type of project, but we as web designers need to seriously consider burning design documentation into our workflow and making it part of the whole design package. It should be part of every design budget. Web design is system design.

The web offers advantages over printed manuals. For one, browser-based manuals cost less to make. They might not cost much less to *design* (although unfortunately I find many web-based design guidelines to be less well-designed than their printed counterparts), but they cost much less to produce. I mean, you don't have to *print and produce a book*. When changes or additions are made to the design system, these web-based design guidelines can be quickly, easily, and cheaply updated with the newest information (**Figure 11.1**). Why printed manuals even exist anymore is beyond my comprehension, except maybe for their own sake. After all, traditionally, many of the printed manuals are beautiful objects in and of themselves.

Another advantage that the web offers is that it's easy to provide and link to design assets. Creating an ad? Choose *Advertising* from a menu, read how ads are constructed, and download the necessary materials. Since all print design workflow is now digital, all kinds of assets can be offered online, from logos and layout grid templates to color profiles and prepress application settings.

---

1 Anna Debenham, "Front-end Style Guides", *24 Ways,* http://24ways.org/2011/front-end-style-guides.

Figure 11.1
Design guidelines on the web, such as this style guide for Drupal.org by Mark Boulton Design, offer many advantages compared to printed manuals.

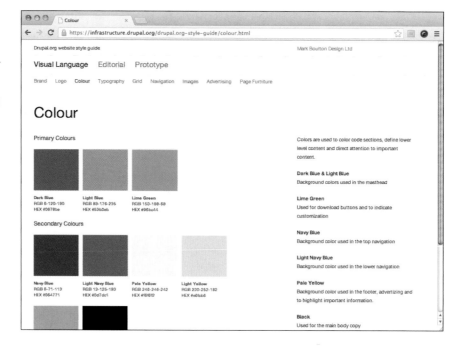

The same goes for websites. In addition to the basic rules of the design system, assets such as icons, fonts, imagery, and CSS snippets can be made available for use by designers.

The main reason I include the creation of design documentation in the responsive workflow is that web-based mockups, while sufficient for communicating the basics of a design to clients and developers, are not sufficient for communicating a design *system*. The mockups show only specific applications of the system; they neither explain the system itself, nor show how to use that system to create *other* applications. This is why I often say that web-based mockups and design documentation *together* are the dynamic duo of the new workflow and are a potential replacement for Photoshop comps. Though to be honest, I never really felt that Photoshop comps alone were enough to communicate a system, either.

Web-based design documentation can do this. But we have to write it first.

The content and structure of design guidelines

There are no real guidelines to creating guidelines, though every designer who has made them could probably come up with his own. Massimo Vignelli's *New York Transit Authority Graphics Standards Manual* (1970) is one of my favorites (**Figure 11.2**). By looking through the table of contents you can see that it's really tailor-made to the project.[2]

This will be true for you as well, but here are some topics to *consider* including in your design guidelines, depending on their relevance to your project and the project scope:

- Design philosophy/background information

- Layout/grid system

- Typography

- Color and texture

- Imagery (whether illustrative or photographic)

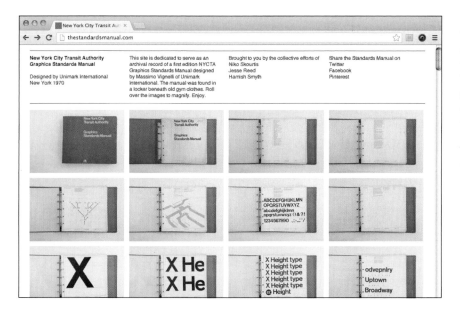

Figure 11.2
This 1970 design standards manual for the New York City Transit Authority shows how content can cater to specific use cases.

2 http://thestandardsmanual.com

This format is used for the table of contents in some manuals. However, it's completely acceptable (and perhaps more logical) to cover these topics, but *structure* your manual according to the sections or components of a website.

The idea is to describe the available design elements, explain *when* it's appropriate to use them, and show *how* to use them in those situations. It's like, "You can use these types of pieces to build a model airplane. Here's how to do that."

When creating your own guidelines, don't grab someone else's table of contents: closely examine the needs of your project and the materials you've created for it. There are no set rules.

Websites are different

It's very possible that, when you create design guidelines for your website, you'll have a section about the color palette and how to use it. This color palette will be used in many places, however, so you'll want to document how the various colors should appear in a specific context. For example, you might write a section about links and buttons, and show the color usage there in addition to the general overview of color. In the end, *which* colors are important, but *where and how they should be used* is more important.

Set up a structure that makes sense for your particular project. You'll also want to choose whether your guidelines will consist of a (perhaps fairly long) one-page document or become a small website in and of itself. You'll need to decide

GUIDELINES COMMUNICATE WHAT YOUR MOCKUP CANNOT

I'm sometimes asked why I choose to create guidelines when I already have design mockups in code. After all, developers can just open up their developer tools and see what color that button is, right?

That's true. Developers can do that, but your client probably won't. Coworkers and future designers who work on the project might not. Besides, the fact that you can see what color a button is and what certain margins are tells you nothing about the *rules* for their use; it's hard to extract systems like variations in layout grid systems just by poking around in developer tools. Guidelines have their place; they are human-readable and, when well-written, easy to understand.

whether or not you need a table of contents, with each item linking to its corresponding section. There is no right or wrong. The most important thing is that your guidelines *communicate* and thus aid in consistency and collaboration.

My wish list for design guideline software

The easiest way to create guidelines for websites is with software. I don't mean use a word processor or anything else you might type into. The easiest way to explain what I mean is to reveal my wish list for web-based design documentation software.

1. **It should be freeform writable.**

   A lot of *documentation software* requires you to do weird things like write all your documentation as comments in the source code itself. I find this nonintuitive and restrictive. I want to be able to simply write a document in a plain text format such as Markdown, and be able to place images, HTML, or code in there when necessary.

2. **Taking of screenshots should be automated.**

   Ideally, a good documentation system would let me choose between adding live HTML examples or screenshots. I tend to use screenshots more often, as I know *exactly* what the reader of the guidelines is seeing. For a given project, you might have tens or hundreds of screenshots. I really don't want to make those by hand—having to do a number of them again each time a change is made. I want this to be an automated process.

3. **Code snippets should update themselves when the mockup changes.**

   Similar to screenshots, I want the code in the documentation to be updated whenever I make changes to the mockup. See the sidebar for why I use code in design guidelines in the first place.

4. **Elements and components should be extracted from the mockups.**

   Some toolkits for creating style guides and pattern libraries require you to put each element or group of elements into separate files. If a site has many elements this is a maintainability issue. I would find it much easier to extract each element I want to document straight from a mockup and have that code placed into my documentation at the appropriate spot.

5. **Code snippets should be syntax highlighted.**

   Syntax highlighting makes code easier to read and understand. Your clients might just gloss over code snippets, but developers who have to create new pages based on your design will have a much easier time of it if your code is easy to read. In fact, with relatively easy-to-understand languages like CSS, syntax highlighting can even enable nontechnical people to understand what the code means. While not an absolute necessity, syntax-highlighting libraries are available and they're a nice thing to have.

I haven't found a single piece of software that does all of these things out of the box. But remember how we used Dexy in Chapter 8, "Creating a Web-Based Mockup," to create our mockups? I use Dexy for design guidelines, too. In fact, design documentation is the reason I started using Dexy in the first place; that I could also use it for mockups was just a bonus, and allowed me to keep my toolset smaller by using the same tool for different things. While Dexy doesn't do everything I want, it utilizes other software applications through its filters. This gives me all the functionality I currently want and more.

WHY I USE CODE IN DESIGN GUIDELINES

I usually show CSS code in my design guidelines. My main purpose is to save time, since I've already spent time defining styles in the mockups; I don't have to do it again when writing guidelines.

I begin with client-friendly material about a given element, followed by a screenshot of what it looks like and a piece of CSS code that describes the properties that create that appearance. Although clients and other nontechnical people are usually only interested in the general description and the screenshot, if they want to know the specific amount of padding on a given element they can fairly easily read the CSS.

An advantage of this approach is that the CSS code can be *automatically updated* when a mockup is updated, meaning that while the general element description often remains the same, I don't have to go back and manually change properties and values.

CSS in documentation is a great alternative to what developers have to do when receiving Photoshop comps: open them up and start measuring things. Showing CSS also allows you to show exactly which elements change at given breakpoints. It's a more effective way of describing aspects of a responsive design.

Using code is not a requirement. I do it, but not for every element and not for every project. Some projects might need only a couple of screenshots and a bit of text.

Creating your design documentation

Now let's walk through the process of creating design guidelines using Dexy. Once you get the hang of it, you can tweak it to suit your taste. For now, just relax and follow along. The process for creating your design guidelines is remarkably similar to how you created your mockup in Chapter 8.

First, in the command line, move into your project folder and run:

```
$ dexy setup
```

Now Dexy is ready to run when you need it, and Dexy's *artifacts* and *logs* folders have been created (you don't need to worry about these; Dexy uses them).

As with the mockups, I prefer my files to contain only the main content, and keep the header and footer in separate files. I could have run the same dexy gen command I ran in Chapter 8, but since the example design guidelines will be very simple (a single web page), we'll just create a simple header and footer by hand. Start with the header. Create a file called _header.html in your project folder. The content of this file will be almost identical to the content of the template we made for use with Pandoc in Chapter 4, "Designing in Text":

```
<!DOCTYPE html>
<html lang="en">
    <head>
        <meta charset="utf-8">
        <meta name="viewport" content="width=device-width,
        →initial-scale=1">
        <title>Design Guidelines</title>
        <link rel="stylesheet" href="styles/guidelines.css"
        →media="screen">

    </head>
    <body>
```

You can probably guess that you'll also need to create a file called `_footer.html`. And indeed, this will contain the following content:

```
    </body>
  </html>
```

Now that you have a header and a footer, you need a file for the main content of the style guidelines. You could just call this `guidelines.markdown`. That's simple and clear: this is the place for the design guidelines. Go ahead and make this file now, which will sit in the project folder along with `_header.html` and `_footer.html`. Later, Dexy will combine these three files to create a single HTML file containing the design guidelines.

NOTE
If you want a design manual with multiple pages, you can set up Dexy with the same approach as in Chapter 8, using the `rdw:mockup` template. The templates are more complex, but the idea is similar. Also, keep an eye on responsivedesign-workflow.com, as new templates may be added in the future and existing ones updated.

Writing the documentation

No matter what tools and tricks you use, software can't write the documentation for you. Writing is the *hard* part. It's the *important* part of documentation. Well-written documentation makes software easy to use. It makes design guidelines easy to follow and thus makes designs easer to implement. It improves communication within the team. Spend plenty of time on getting it right. The writing should be the main part of your documentation.

Style guides are not novels, and most people won't read them from cover to cover, so to speak, so make sure nothing's hidden. Think about what situations your reader might be confronted with that would lead them to consult your guide. Provide basic principles for using your designs as well as detailed information for the various situations you think up. Repetition and cross-references are fine and encouraged.

Examples are great, and a lot of this chapter focuses on automating the inclusion of examples in your design documentation. Please don't think that this focus means examples are more important. They're not. Examples, such as screenshots and code snippets and even live, working code, are simply aids to understanding well-written text.

I recommend starting with this content as well, in much the same way I recommend starting the responsive design workflow with content. *Content first* counts just as much for design guidelines as it does for your mockups.

It could be that this content is not written by you. This is one good reason to use Markdown: anyone with five minutes of training can write content in Markdown. The actual text might be written after the design is created, but if you or a fellow designer is writing it, it might be written *during* the making of the design. In my experience, it's both: some parts of the guidelines are written during the design phase (such as philosophy and background information) and some parts are written after the mockups have been completed (mainly because that's when the client has approved everything and you know it's safe to include).

Either way, `guidelines.markdown` is where this documentation will go, if you're creating a one-page doc as we're doing in the example for this chapter. You'll be creating guidelines that describe the design in your mockups, but let's create a really simple document just to understand how all the pieces fit together. First, put a little bit of text into the Markdown file:

```
# Responsive Design Workflow book site: design guidelines

This page contains the design standards used in creating the
book site. These guidelines can be used to create subsequent
pages or other web projects related to the book.

## Background

The site has been designed to be a companion to the book, in
terms of both visuals and content. The basic color palette,
typography, and other aspects of the book's design language
have been ported to the web, while attempting to remain
consistent with the look and feel of the book. The biggest
difference between the book site and the design of the book
itself is in regard to layout: the website uses a respon-
sive approach, in which the layout may change depending on
the size of the user's screen. Content remains consistent
regardless of the device.

## Responsiveness and breakpoints

There are three major breakpoints for the page layout:
`400px`, `600px` and `900px`. The following examples show
how the website looks at these three viewport widths:
```

Now we come to the point when an example must be inserted. It might not be desirable to stop at every example, so while writing, simply insert a placeholder where you want to put the example, something like:

```
[[INSERT SCREENSHOTS HERE]]
```

You can then go back and add your examples later.

Inserting example material

There are many different types of examples you might use in your documentation:

◆ Illustrations, such as breakpoint graphs

◆ Screenshots of whole pages or specific sections or elements

◆ Actual code, such as a block of CSS

◆ Actual rendered code, like an actual button or animation

Of course, you can include anything you would in HTML, such as video. Remember that Markdown is a front end for HTML, so you're allowed to use HTML in your Markdown, should you wish to do so.

Continuing with the example documentation above, we want to include three screenshots of the page, one at each major breakpoint. Luckily we already have the screenshots we made in Chapter 9, "Presentation, Round One: Screenshots." So to get these into the documentation, we need only link to them:

```
![](/mockup/screenshots/home400.png)
![](/mockup/screenshots/home600.png)
![](/mockup/screenshots/home900.png)
```

This is exactly the same effect as using the `<img>` element in HTML: it simply pulls in an existing image. We can use the power of Dexy combined with CasperJS to create screenshots of everything we need, pulling them into the documentation at the placeholders automatically. This gives us the advantage of not having to change anything by hand if edits are made in the original

NOTE

Pixels are used here for consistency with our example breakpoints when we took screenshots in Chapter 9. If you took your screenshots using other units like ems, then by all means use those here as well.

design; running Dexy will take care of updating the screenshot and inserting it into the documentation.

Let's try it out.

Creating screenshots

To create the screenshots in this example, you'll need a slightly modified version of the script you made to take screenshots for presentation mockups in Chapter 9. You can either make a copy of that screenshot script (in your mockup folder) and put it in your project folder, or you can make a new one. You can keep the name screenshots.js, as this won't conflict with the one in your mockup folder. The script should look like this:

```
var casper = require('casper').create();

casper.start();

var baseUrl = 'http://localhost:8085'; // <- Should be the
  →host Dexy names when running "dexy serve"
var breakpoints = [400, 600, 900];

casper.open(baseUrl).then(function () {
    breakpoints.forEach(function(breakpoint) {
        casper.viewport(breakpoint, 800).capture('images/' +
          →breakpoint + '.png', {
        top: 0,
        left: 0,
        width: breakpoint,
        height: casper.evaluate(function(){ return
          →document.body.scrollHeight; })
        });
    });
});

casper.run();
```

This one is a lot simpler, because we don't have to loop through a list of pages. (If you decide that you want that, then you could simply use the same script we used in Chapter 9.) This script opens up the home page of the mockup that's being served via `dexy serve` and takes a screenshot at each of the breakpoints in the breakpoints array. The name of the saved file is `[breakpoint].png` and the file is placed in the *images* folder. So we have to change the links in the Markdown document:

```
![](images/400.png)
![](images/600.png)
![](images/900.png)
```

It's that short and sweet. Now in order to get Dexy to run the CasperJS script, we have to tell it what to do by using a `dexy.yaml` file.

Making the Dexy configuration file

Dexy reads a configuration file so it knows what to do. This file is required for every Dexy project. Make a new, empty file in your project folder and call it `dexy.yaml`. We'll walk through the creation of this file step by step. First, let's tell Dexy what we want to happen to guidelines.markdown:

```
guidelines.markdown|pandoc|hd|ft:
    - partials
    - screenshots
```

Here, we're saying, "Run `guidelines.markdown` through Pandoc, then Dexy's header (hd) filter, then Dexy's footer (ft) filter. The file utilizes *partials* and *screenshots*." Right now, Dexy doesn't know what partials are (they're the files we're using as a header and a footer, and we're just calling them *partials*) or where the screenshots are:

```
guidelines.markdown|pandoc|hd|ft:
    - partials
    - screenshots
partials:
    - _*.html
```

This last line tells Dexy that a *partial* is any file in the project folder that starts with an underscore and ends with the extension `.html`, in this case, the header and footer files. Next, we have to tell Dexy about the screenshots:

```
guidelines.markdown|pandoc|hd|ft:
    - partials
    - screenshots
partials:
    - _*.html
screenshots:
    - screenshots.js|casperjs
```

This says to run `screenshots.js` through `casperjs`. Now we should be good to go. Save this whole thing and we'll test the project.

Testing your Dexy project

Since you want to take screenshots of your mockup, you need to run `dexy serve` from within the mockup folder. But you will also need to run Dexy while you're doing that. Since that's not possible to do in one terminal, you'll need to either use a tool like GNU Screen if you're familiar with it or open a new terminal (in a new tab or a new window; either is fine). In one terminal, navigate to your mockup folder (the one that also contains a `dexy.yaml` you made in Chapter 8) and run `dexy serve`. Go to the address Dexy gives you in a browser to confirm that it's working. If so, then switch to the other terminal, make sure you're in the folder with `guidelines.markdown`, and run `dexy`.

Dexy should complete within a few seconds. If you look in your project folder, you'll see that Dexy added an *output* folder. Open that folder, and you'll see some files and an images folder. The file `guidelines.html` is the design guidelines web page Dexy generated for you. Open the file in a browser and take a look (**Figure 11.3**). It's not pretty yet, but you can see that Dexy has:

◆ Converted the Markdown content to HTML

◆ Created the screenshots that are called up by the converted HTML content

◆ Wrapped the converted HTML content with a header and a footer, creating a proper web page

Figure 11.3
Dexy has generated an unstyled HTML document from Markdown content and created and imported screenshots.

The guidelines document still needs styling of its own (we already prepared for that by linking to `guidelines.css` in `_header.html`; you can make this file and use it to style your guidelines doc), and will also require more content. There's no need to create a complete style guide out of our example, but let's do just enough to show you how to include screenshots of specific page elements, live HTML from your mockup, and pieces of code.

Taking screenshots of specific elements

You now know how to insert screenshots of whole pages into your design documentation. But what if you only want to include part of a page? Remember that Dexy isn't actually taking screenshots; it's running CasperJS for you. This means that all the screenshots you want to take and how you want to take them are determined by `screenshots.js`. Let's see how we can use CasperJS's `captureSelector()` function to capture screenshots of specific elements.

Until now, we've been using the `capture()` function, which captures a whole page. `captureSelector()` takes a selector as an argument and captures only the selected element. This can be extremely useful, and by combining the breakpoint looping we've been doing with `captureSelector()`, it's even possible to take screenshots of specific elements *when the page is at different widths*. For now, let's just grab an image of the h1 heading from the page. First,

NOTE

There's a lot you can do with CasperJS, so for the really fancy stuff I must refer you to the CasperJS documentation (which is quite clearly written), as the details are outside the scope of this book. See http://casperjs.org/.

we need to add some content to the documentation, since we're talking about the heading. Under the images you added earlier, add some text about the h1:

```
![](images/400.png)
![](images/600.png)
![](images/900.png)

## The main heading

The main heading of the page is also the title of the book,
→and has a different appearance than normal headings:

![](images/h1.png)
```

I think you know where we're going with this. We need to adjust screenshots.js so it will capture a shot of the heading in addition to the full-page screenshots we already have.

Add the desired screenshot to screenshots.js using the captureSelector() function:

```
casper.open(baseUrl).then(function () {
    breakpoints.forEach(function(breakpoint) {
        casper.viewport(breakpoint, 800).capture('images/' +
        →breakpoint + '.png', {
            top: 0,
            left: 0,
            width: breakpoint,
            height: casper.evaluate(function(){ return
            →document.body.scrollHeight; })
        });
    });
});

casper.then(function() {
    this.captureSelector('images/h1.png', 'h1');
});

casper.run();
```

NOTE

You'll have to add something to screenshots.js for every screenshot you want, but you'll usually have to do it only once. Remember, if your mockup changes, then your changes will be in new screenshots in the updated documentation when you run Dexy again!

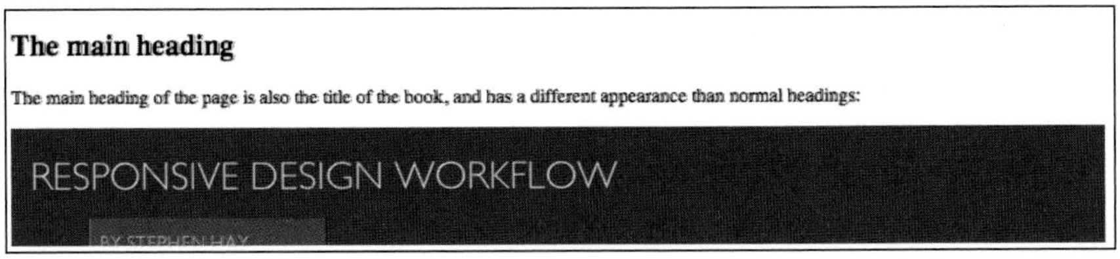

Figure 11.4
Using CasperJS with
Dexy makes it easy to
include screenshots of
specific elements.

Figure 11.4
Using CasperJS with Dexy makes it easy to include screenshots of specific elements.

The function takes two arguments: the name of the file to be saved and the selector, in this case simply `h1`. If you're familiar with CSS selectors, you know everything you need to know: `#foo` will select the element with an `id` of foo. CasperJS will even allow XPath expressions, if you prefer.

Look carefully at that `casper.then()` function block we just added. To make things easy to change, if I need screenshots of 20 different elements, I'll simply place 20 of these function blocks under one another, each capturing a different element. It won't win you any JavaScript awards, but hey, we're making design guidelines, not a mission-critical JavaScript app.

Now run `dexy -r`, which resets Dexy and runs it again. When you open `guidelines.html`, you should see the text about the heading and the screenshot included (**Figure 11.4**).

Including rendered HTML

Sometimes you might want to have actual working, rendered code show up in the browser as part of your design guidelines. For example, you might have a button that has a certain hover effect, and you don't feel that a screenshot is sufficient. Adding this kind of code is possible, and one way to do it is to use Dexy's `htmlsections` filter (yes, Dexy has *a lot* of filters, and you can even make your own).

I don't do this often. We already have mockups that contain these elements if someone needs to hover above a button. It's good practice to link to the mockup from the design documentation anyway. In fact, the mockups are, in my opinion, an essential *part* of the design documentation.

Inserting rendered HTML into your docs takes more time than screenshots, because you need to place special comments in the mockup surrounding the parts you want to extract. Not only that, but unless you use the same CSS for both your design docs and your mockup, you'll need to devise your own method of styling the elements you import, since they won't have the mockup styling by default. However, should you want to do it, here's how.

To keep the example simple, let's say you don't want a *screenshot* of the h1, but you want *the actual* h1 in your docs. You need to tell Dexy that the h1 is what you want. Open the mockup HTML file from which you want to extract the h1, and add comments above and below the code you want to extract:

```
<!-- section "h1" -->
<h1>Responsive Design Workflow</h1>
<!-- section "end" -->
```

Then you need to adjust your `dexy.yaml` file to tell it to run your mockup HTML through the `htmlsections` filter:

```
guidelines.markdown|pandoc|hd|ft|jinja:
    - partials
    - screenshots
    - sources
partials:
    - _*.html
screenshots:
    - screenshots.js|casperjs
sources:
    - mockup/output-site/index.html|htmlsections
```

Here we've added a new input source for the guidelines document, from which we'll extract the HTML we want. You can't call up the h1 in the same way you called up an image. For this, you're going to use a Jinja snippet. Dexy offers a way to see which snippets are available: the dexy viewer (**Figure 11.5**). Start by running Dexy again so your changes are processed:

```
$ dexy -r
```

Now run:

```
$ dexy viewer
```

NOTE

If you use `htmlsections` to pull out HTML code for rendering and you add the special comments to your Dexy-generated mockup file, they'll disappear when you update your mockup. You'll need to add the comments to your original markdown file and run `dexy -r` in your mockup folder first, then move to your project folder and run `dexy -r` there as well.

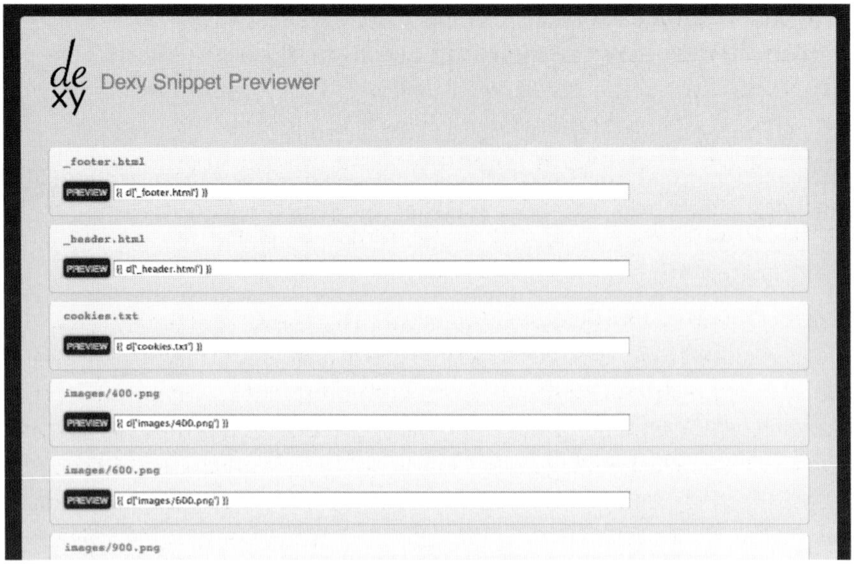

Figure 11.5
Dexy's handy snippet previewer (`dexy viewer`) makes it easy to find the Jinja snippets you need to copy and paste them into your docs.

This will return a URL that you can open in your browser. You'll see a page with a bunch of Jinja snippets; look for the `htmlsections` snippets. Copy the h1 snippet and paste it into your `guidelines.markdown` file:

```
{{ d['mockup/output-site/index.html|htmlsections']['h1'] }}
```

This works the same way as pulling in an image, only now it pulls in the HTML snippet. Run `dexy -r` again and open the `guidelines.html` document again (or refresh). You should now see the actual h1 at the bottom of the page.

It might take some getting used to the process, but you can see how easy it is to pull screenshots or HTML snippets into your documentation.

Now let's look at how to pull another useful type of information into your design documentation: code.

Including syntax-highlighted code

There are many reasons you might want to include actual code in your design docs. You might have sections of your document in which you explain and annotate code from your website or application, CSS to complete the description of an element, code for the reader to copy and paste, or live examples of running code with the corresponding code displayed.

As mentioned, for each element I import CSS snippets in addition to a high-level description and screenshot. For example, next to a screenshot of the `h1`, I'll import and display the CSS to show which styles apply to `h1`. The CSS provides a very specific description of how the `h1` is styled. It might seem quite technical to use CSS in this way, but depending on how you write your CSS, it can be a very effective way to describe the visual rules that should be applied to an element. `margin: 1em;` is almost as understandable as, "The `h1` must have a margin of `1em` applied to it."

Of course, you might choose to display only a high-level description of the visual rules of an element, but make the CSS available specifically for those looking for the styles that should be applied to display the element properly. Since the documentation is a plain HTML document, you can do anything you want with it, such as adding a bit of JavaScript to collapse these CSS code snippets so that nontechnical readers aren't directly confronted with them. Interested readers can expand the snippets. That's one of the great things about using web technology and tools like Dexy: you can completely tailor your own workflow.

In much the same way you can import code to render, you can import raw code to display. You still need to tell Dexy which code snippets you want to import. The syntax is slightly different than when we used the `htmlsections` filter. For importing CSS code, we'll be using the `idiopidae` filter, which I'll refer to as `idio`.

`idio` lets you cut code into sections by adding comments in the code. It works for many languages. To use it in your CSS, open your mockup's CSS file and add comments surrounding each section you want to pull into your design doc, like this:

```css
/*** @export "h1" css */
h1 {
    text-transform: uppercase;
    background-color: #45565c;
    color: #fee29d;
    margin-top: 0;
    padding: .5em;
}
/*** @end */
```

Notice in the code above that you define an export by using `@export` `"[name]"`, and ending it with `@end`. If the code blocks you're using immediately follow each other, the start of a new code block implies the end of the previous, so in that case you can omit the `@end`. Just keep in mind that Dexy counts everything following an `@export` as a code block to be exported until it finds either a new block or an `@end`.

It's important to use three asterisks to start your comments. Also, at the time of this writing, you're required to add the name of the language after the name of your snippet; in this case, that's CSS, of course. Depending on the code language, `idio` also works with single-line comment syntax, such as:

> /// `@export` `"foo"` *(does not work with CSS)*

Go ahead and delineate a single code block in your mockup's CSS using `idio` comments, as I've done above. Save the file. Now, as you might have guessed, we have to tell `dexy.yaml` that we're using `idio` for CSS, and we have to indicate that we'll be using yet another input source for our `guidelines.markdown` file:

```
guidelines.markdown|pandoc|hd|ft|jinja:
    - partials
    - screenshots
    - sources
partials:
    - _*.html
screenshots:
    - screenshots.js|casperjs
sources:
    - mockup/output-site/index.html|htmlsections
    - mockup/styles/base.css|idio
```

Run `dexy -r` and then `dexy viewer`, then open the browser to the URL Dexy displays. You should see an updated snippets page, with a section for your CSS. Find the snippet with `h1` in it and paste that into your `guidelines.markdown` file at the bottom:

```
{{ d['mockup/styles/base.css|idio']['h1'] }}
```

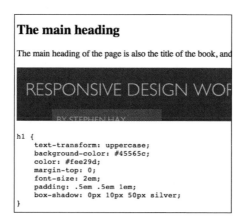

Figure 11.6
Dexy makes it easy to incorporate code from other files into your style guide.

You'll probably recognize by now that this snippet will pull in this particular bit of CSS at this spot in your document. Try it out by running dexy -r again and then opening the resulting guidelines.html file (or refreshing the one you had open) in your browser. When you scroll down to the bottom, you should see a bit of CSS code with the h1 styles (**Figure 11.6**).

This is already pretty cool; we can pull in screenshots or actual HTML of an element, and we can pull in the CSS that describes the styles of that element. If we do this for most or all of our elements, we have put all the moving parts in place to generate a good portion of our design documentation on the fly. When you make a change in your mockup, run dexy -r again and voilà, you have updated documentation. Both screenshots and code are updated.

Now you've got this CSS code in your docs, but it's all black. It would be nice to syntax highlight this code. Because of the idio comments we used in the CSS, idio knows we're pulling in CSS code. idio also supports syntax highlighting out of the box, using Python's Pygments syntax highlighting library.[3] To take advantage of this, let's edit _header.html and a little bit of Jinja that will pull in a syntax highlighting style sheet. Put the following in the <head> element:

```
<style>
    {{pygments['pastie.css']}}
</style>
```

3 http://pygments.org

NOTE
You may have noticed a dexy.yaml in your mockup folder and one in your main project folder. To update your design documentation and create a new guidelines.html, run dexy -r in the project folder. To update your mockup, run dexy -r in your mockup folder. Dexy reads the YAML file from the folder from which you run it and acts accordingly.

Figure 11.7
Syntax highlighting code is easy and makes your included code easy to read.

Save the file. Here you can see that we're inserting a Pygments style sheet called `pastie.css`. This gives us highlighting in certain colors. There are other style sheets to choose from; you can find out more at the Pygments website. For now, just use `pastie.css`. Now run `dexy -r` again and refresh `guidelines.html` again. Scroll down and look at the CSS. It's syntax highlighted (**Figure 11.7**)!

Making the documentation your own

When creating your own documentation (your own *style guide*, if you will), you'll want to design *it* as well. It's a normal web page, so you can link to your own style guide CSS from within `_header.html` (**Figure 11.8**). You can add scripts, a table of contents, and anything else you need. You can create a multipage style guide by doing everything we've discussed above, but using the `rdw:mockup` template as we did with the mockup instead of the single markdown file we used in this example.

It can take a little while to wrap your head around the way Dexy works and keep track of the moving parts. The key is to do as we've done in this chapter: start with a simple Markdown file, add the header and footer, and slowly add and try out each piece to see how it works.

And by all means, if you like doing your style guides in Word, InDesign, or PowerPoint, more power to ya (but you might see me out having fun while you're still updating your docs by hand). This chapter presented some of the building blocks you can use to automate a good portion of your design documentation. It's up to you to take it where you want it to go.

Figure 11.8
Since the style guide is just HTML, it's easy to add your own style to make your docs fit your client's brand.

Now it's time to go

This marks the end of this book, how I end my responsive design workflow. It also marks a beginning: the beginning of your own experimentation. You might feel comfortable with the entire workflow. On the other hand, maybe you are very happy with your own current workflow, but perhaps find one or two ideas in this book that could be useful additions to your own way of doing things. You might know of other tools to accomplish the same things I've done here, or even better, you might build some of these tools.

You might do as I've done and find tools that were originally designed for other purposes, and use them for your *own* purposes. Some parts of this workflow might come across as too much too soon; many people have an aversion to using web technology as a design tool. Some will embrace it, as I have, though truthfully it did take me a while; I had the same aversion!

So turn the page and you'll see, one last time, the steps in this workflow:

1. Create a content inventory (Chapter 2).

2. Make content reference wireframes (Chapter 3).

3. Design in structured text (Chapter 4).

4. Create a linear design (Chapter 5).

5. Determine breakpoints and document them using breakpoint graphs (Chapter 6).

6. Sketch and develop designs for the major breakpoints (Chapter 7).

7. Develop a web-based mockup of your design (Chapter 8).

8. Take and present screenshots of your design as your initial design presentation (Chapter 9).

9. Present and iterate on your web-based mockup for subsequent presentations (Chapter 10).

10. Create a style guide (Chapter 11).

When you've completed these steps and gotten your client's approval, you can hand over your deliverables and be confident that you've done work that keeps the medium in mind, is based on structured content, embraces progressive enhancement, and is rooted in the responsive nature of the web.

As creative legend Paul Arden said,

"If you can't solve a problem, it's because you're playing by the rules."

Find out which web design rules aren't working for you.

Then go break them.

Index